Key History
for GCSE

International Relations 1919–39

TEACHER'S GUIDE

Keith Shephard

Stanley Thornes (Publishers) Ltd

First published in 1998 by:
Stanley Thornes (Publishers) Ltd
Ellenborough House
Wellington Street
CHELTENHAM GL50 1YW
England

98 99 00 01 02 / 10 9 8 7 6 5 4 3 2 1

A catalogue record for this book is available from the British Library.

ISBN 0-7487-3484-8

Printed and bound in Great Britain at Ashford Colour Press, Gosport.

Contents

Introduction: Practical advice on how to use the *International Relations 1919–39* pupils' book and teacher's guide   **4**

GSCE syllabus matching guide   **11**

Worksheets 1–34

1   Overview

2   International relations 1919–41

3   Governments

4   Solving the causes of the war

5   The Peacemakers

6   The reshaping of Europe at Versailles

7   The Treaty of Versailles – The views of historians

8   Justifying the Treaty of Versailles (1)

9   Justifying the Treaty of Versailles (2)

10   The other Peace Treaties

11   Future trouble spots?

12   War debts and reparations

13   Treaties and pacts in the 1920s

14   France searches for security

15   Britain and the world 1919–33

16   The USA and isolationism

17   Germany and Versailles

18   The League of Nations – Organisation

19   The League of Nations – Powers, weaknesses and strengths

20   The League of Nations in the 1920s

21   The League of Nations and Abyssinia

22   Steps to war 1933–39 (1)

23   Steps to war 1933–39 (2)

24   The fall of Czechoslovakia

25   Appeasement

26   The Nazi-Soviet Pact

27   The causes of war – Interpretations

28   The causes of war

29   World peace 1919–39

30   Russia and international relations 1919–41

31   The USA and international relations 1919–41

32   Japan and international relations 1919–41

33   Timeline between the wars

34   Hitler's responsibility

Introduction

The story of international relations between 1919 and 1939 is a hectic and fascinating one which includes most of the issues and problems usually present in relations between countries. It is not a particularly easy subject for students as it covers a wide range of countries, statesmen, political philosophies and concepts such as appeasement. The chronology can also cause problems with significant events and developments occurring at the same time.

This topic does, however, have a more immediate relevance to students today than some History topics they may study. The extent to which things have changed and whether similar problems exist today is referred to in the 'discussion points' in the section on practical advice. Issues such as appeasement, disarmament, democracy, nationalism, economic depression and even communism and fascism are still with us somewhere in the world.

A key feature of the pupils' book is to help students understand the issues by involving them in decision-making exercises based on the decisions which faced statesmen. Such exercises are found in the following sections:

Solving the causes of the war, pages 10–11
Justifying the Treaty of Versailles, pages 22–23
Britain and the world 1919–33, pages 36–37
The League of Nations, pages 48–51
Abyssinia and the League, pages 66–68
Steps to war 1933–39, pages 72–81.

Other features include profile boxes of the main statesmen and extensive use of cartoons, maps and artwork to illustrate concepts and problems. You may wish to tackle some of the topics in a different order to that in the book. Some topics, in particular disarmament and events in the Far East, may be better dealt with in one go. This route together with page numbers is mentioned in the following section.

Practical advice on how to use the pupils' book

This section provides:
a) A brief statement of the content of the units.
b) Some background information to some of the sources and events.
c) For ease of reference, some of the answers to some of the questions and exercises.
d) Teaching ideas. Many of these are obvious and experienced teachers will be familiar with many of them – they are aimed primarily at newly qualified teachers.
3) Discussion points. The aim of these is to emphasise the contemporary nature of the issues in this period.

Most of the worksheets are designed to be used with lower ability pupils, although some, for example worksheets 9, 28 and 34, are considerably more difficult. There are two types of worksheets. Some are simply to help students organise their answers to specific questions or exercises in the pupils' book – some of these are copies of sources and maps. Others provide additional information and tasks.

1 Europe and the world in 1918

Introduction (pages 4–5)

This provides an overview of the period showing the main events, developments and statesmen, and is intended to remind students of their work on 'The Twentieth-century World' in Key Stage 3. Source **B** shows some of the straightforward links between the wars. To show the complexity of causation, links could be added between the boxes, for example a 'reparations line' linking the Peace Treaties with the Depression. Worksheet 1 is a copy of Source **B**.

The last paragraph on page 5 of the pupils' book poses a number of questions about causation which link the two world wars. Discussing these should show that a number of other events were also necessary, for example there were other reasons besides the Depression which enabled Hitler to come to power.

Worksheet 2 is a copy of Source **C**.

Teaching ideas:
- There are many difficult terms on these pages which are explained later in the book. Pupils could be asked to identify such terms and begin to compile a glossary.
- Blank out some key words on Worksheet 1 and ask students to fill the gaps.

Revolution in Russia (pages 6–7)

This spread introduces students to the ideas of communism and capitalism with a reasonably simple explanation. An understanding of this is crucial, particularly when considering the final steps to war and the events of 1939–41.

Teaching idea: Begin by discussing Sources **C** and **D** and the problems such differences might cause.

Discussion point: What happened to communism in Russia?

New ideas and old ideas (pages 8–9)

This unit is linked to Revolution in Russia. An understanding of the political spectrum is vital and teachers will know how difficult some students find this. Source **B** shows the changes which took place before 1939. Worksheet 3 asks students to use page 8 to complete a simple colouring chart showing these changes. If students are keeping a glossary, the terms in this unit can be added. The aim of Source **D** is to show the similarity of method of communist and fascist regimes but to highlight the key differences also.

The quotations in Question 3 are a) Mussolini, b) Karl Marx, c) F D Roosevelt.
Discussion point: Which countries are still communist today?

Solving the causes of the war (pages 10–11)

This exercise asks students to solve some of the key causes of the First World War before they study the attempts to deal with these problems in the Peace Treaties and the inter-war years. Worksheet 4 provides a framework for their answers.
Discussion point: Do any of these problems still cause trouble today? How? Why have they not been solved?

The world outside Europe (pages 12–13)

This unit introduces the problems outside Europe which were to contribute to the breakdown in international relations. Students are asked to identify possible problems using Source **A**. Hopefully they will identify Britain's territories in the Far East, and China, Abyssinia and Japan as the problems. The emphasis is on the power of the USA and whether she would want to become involved in such problems. Having identified the problems it is worth returning to the question of whether the USA would want to act as peacemaker for the world – this helps to introduce the idea of isolationism.
Teaching idea: A class vote from the point of view of Americans: 'Should the USA act as world peacemaker?'
Discussion point: What happened to the empires of the European powers? Are there any colonies left?

Memories of war (pages 14–15)

The aim of this unit is to help students to appreciate the kind of emotions people had as the peace settlements approached and the pressure on politicians. The case of Captain Fryatt is interesting, the Germans went to some lengths to capture him. The text for 22 June 1916 is useful for discussing how they captured him – secret agents, etc., and why they went to such effort. See *History Today*, August 1988, for more detail on the incident.
Teaching idea: One way to generate discussion is to tell students you have written down five words describing different emotions and aims caused by the war (for example: revenge, hatred, fear, blame and compensation). Then ask students to work in pairs to select five words and see who comes closest to your five words. Do the words describe different emotions? Can agreement be reached on a final list of five words which best describe feelings? Which emotions apply to which countries?

The Peace Treaties

The Treaty of Versailles – The Peacemakers (pages 16–17)

All the GCSE syllabuses stress the aims of the peacemakers. The intention here is to understand the aims of the peacemakers before considering the terms of the treaties. Students are presented with the main questions which faced the peacemakers, asked to decide on the point of view of each of the 'Big Three' peacemakers and then see how often their leaders agreed. Worksheet 5 is to help students organise their decisions. Worksheet 6 is a copy of Source **B** on which students can record the territory lost by Germany.
Teaching idea: This is a natural topic for group work as many teachers will know, for example groups of three, one student representing each country and a majority decision accepted.
Discussion point: Is it right that the victors in a war decide on the peace terms? What problems might this cause?

The Treaty of Versailles – The terms (pages 18–19)

This unit enables students to compare the terms of Versailles with the aims of each of the 'Big Three'. Worksheet 6 makes use of Source **A** so that students can colour code to show the land lost by Germany.
Teaching idea: Check that students' decisions on Worksheet 5 are correct. Then compare them with the terms on pages 18–19 by highlighting those accepted at Versailles. Which leader was most successful? Which of the terms might be likely to cause problems in the future? What sort of problems?
Discussion point: How do the borders of Germany today compare with those before and after Versailles?

Views on the Treaty of Versailles (pages 20–21)

While German views on the Treaty of Versailles are reasonably uniform (Sources **A–C** are all German), students may have difficulty appreciating that views among the victorious nations varied.
Teaching idea: Group work. Before reading this unit, photocopy and cut out the sources and any others you have expressing views on Versailles, remove any captions and ask each group to sort them according to a) for or against the Treaty, b) nationality of cartoonist or writer.

Justifying the Treaty of Versailles (pages 22–23)

To help students with this difficult concept two opposing views are provided as a prompt for deciding if the aims were reasonable and the terms fair. Worksheet 8 is an expanded version of the chart on page 23 which requires decisions on the territorial changes and provides space for students to add reasons for their answers.

Source **B** is a German cartoon.

Teaching idea: Begin by discussing the idea of justification using contemporary examples, for example the need for homework, a sending-off in a recent soccer match, school punishments. This discussion will usually centre on the guilt of the person involved. Worksheet 9 is for extension work: students may well assume that Germany was responsible for the war and this will influence their views on whether Versailles was justified. What if Britain and France were responsible for the war? Worksheet 9 puts forward the view that Britain and France wanted the war.

The other Peace Treaties (pages 24–25)

This unit and the next can be used to emphasise the idea of national self-determination and the difficulties of drawing national boundaries in areas of mixed populations. The creation of the new states of Czechoslovakia, Poland and Yugoslavia shows this well. Worksheet 10 is an enlarged copy of Source **B** to colour and label. Worksheet 11 asks students to identify possible future trouble spots.

The material on Turkey can be used to discuss the success of President Wilson's aim (in his Fourteen Points) to end empires.

Teaching idea: Start with the map and ask students to identify the countries which are likely to have difficult relations with their neighbours. The pain and suffering caused by ethnic cleansing, such as in Turkey and Greece, will seem remote. Try starting the lesson by re-seating students according to a strict rule, such as girl/boy or alphabetically; and discussing how much worse it might be if they were forced to move school, house, town, country, etc.

Consequences and future problems (pages 26–29)

As in the previous unit these pages can be used to identify future problems, in particular Sources **E** and **F** on page 28.

For ease of reference the answers to the questions on page 27 are:
1 a) For example the Hungarians in the middle of Romania and very small enclaves such as Bulgarians in Romania.

b) This requires students to count every patch of different population on the map; depending on how strictly you count the patches the answer can be 20+.
c) Macedonians, Ukrainians.
d) The enclave of Hungarians in Romania.
e) Yugoslavia.
f) Austria and Czechoslovakia.
g) Sudeten Germans.

2 Hungary.
3 Germans.
4 See Source **B** and perhaps discuss problems today in the former Yugoslavia.

Discussion point: Which of these national groups have their own countries today?

3 The post-war world

War debts and reparations (pages 30–31)

The story of debts and reparations can prove to be a learning trouble spot, particularly the rescheduling of debts in the Dawes Plan and Young Plan, and the fact that the loans were from American banks rather than the US Government. This unit presents a simplified version of a complex situation. The effect of the occupation of the Ruhr on the German economy is covered in Germany and the world 1919–29, pages 40–41. Source **B** is a Dutch cartoon. Worksheet 12 is a matching exercise.

For Question 2 pupils will hopefully recall the events in Russia in 1917.

Teaching idea: Ask students by which year they think Germany had to repay the reparations of £6,600,000. See who is closest to the rescheduled date of 1988 in the Young Plan. Was this fair or ridiculous?

Treaties and pacts in the 1920s (pages 32–33)

The idea of this unit is to present the treaties and pacts in one place for ease of reference.

Worksheet 13 is a wordsearch on the treaties and pacts. The answers are: **1.** disarmament, **2.** Pacific, **3.** USA, **4.** Italy, **5.** Rapallo, **6.** tank, **7.** Europe, **8.** Belgium, **9.** Rhineland, **10.** Poland, **11.** Germany, **12.** Warfare, **13.** Japan, **14.** Locarno.

France searches for security (pages 34–35)

This presents five reasons for French fears and five ways in which France sought security. Worksheet 14 is a game of snakes and ladders, and is simply a fun way of reinforcing this topic.

Source **G** is from *The Illustrated London News*.

Teaching idea: Students cover up 'The search for security' section on page 35 and suggest their own solutions to each of the five reasons. This can lead to some interesting suggestions for Reason 4, although it is unlikely that students will suggest one idea which nearly became law in 1919 – that for every child a father (but not the mother) had he received an extra vote in elections. Students can also place the reasons in order of greatest danger to France – this can help them appreciate the connections between the reasons.

Discussion point: Why does France not have such fears today? Are we concerned about population control today? Why?

4 Countries and problems

Britain and the world 1919–33 (pages 36–37)

The aim of this unit is to introduce students to the policy of appeasement and enable them to appreciate the reasons for the policy in the 1920s. An optimistic view of Britain's position in 1919 is presented, followed by the concerns and problems. Students are then presented with three possible policies and asked to choose one which they think will satisfy as many of the concerns as possible and overcome as many problems as possible.

Discussion of the possible policies should highlight the disadvantages of policies 1 and 2 as well as the dangers of policy 3.

Worksheet 15 is a chart to help students organise their answers when deciding which of the policies Britain should follow.

The USA and isolationism (pages 38–39)

This unit concentrates on the American views of Versailles, but also reminds us that the USA did not retreat totally into isolation. American political parties tend to be something of a learning trouble spot with many students. Worksheet 16 is a matching exercise.

Teaching idea: Use these pages as the basis for a role-play or debate between Wilson and his opponents on whether the USA should sign the Treaty of Versailles and enter the League of Nations. The teacher may need to take the role of Wilson.

Discussion point: Why then did the USA become involved in the Second World War? Does the USA follow a policy of isolationism today? Does this mean she has learnt from experience?

Germany and the world 1919–29 (pages 40–41)

This covers hyperinflation in 1923 and charts the rehabilitation of Germany in the 1920s. Views at the time of the Locarno Treaties are contrasted with more recent reassessments.

Source **A** is a bank note depicting the dance of the death of the financial system. It is from the town of Vohwinkel and lists around the edge the prices of various products on 15 October 1923. Clockwise from the top left these are: one litre of water 98 thousand marks, one pound of salt 42 million, one egg 75 million, one litre of milk 152 million, one pound of potatoes 40 million, one herring 50 million, one pound of bread 210 million, one pound of lard (pork fat) 1¼ billion, one pair of shoes 6 billion, one death certificate 600 million and one coffin 45 billion marks.

Worksheet 17 looks at the immediate impact of the Treaty on Germany (this is a MEG Focus Point).

Teaching idea: Start by looking at Source **A** and Question 1, ask students what is happening and what problems this will cause. Ask students if they can work out any of the products and prices on Source **A**.

Discussion point: Do we have inflation today? What has increased in price that pupils use and was this due to inflation?

Russia and the world 1919–34 (pages 42–43)

It may be advisable to look again at pages 8–9, New ideas and old ideas, to remind students of the communist aim of world revolution.

Teaching idea: Source **C** is a good starting point to gain student interest and discuss problems in Russia. These events can give rise to many questions: Why do people resort to cannibalism? Why was there famine? Who was to blame?

Discussion point: What do students know about the state of Russia's economy today?

Mussolini and Fascist Italy (pages 44–45)

Again it may be necessary to remind students of the beliefs and aims of fascism before tackling this unit.

Discussion point: Would such a man as Mussolini be likely to become Prime Minister of Italy (or Britain) today?

Japan's problems (pages 46–47)

The aim of this unit is a) to provide the background to Japan's expansion in the 1930s and b) to remind students that some of the problems which led to the Second World War were outside Europe.

You may prefer to continue the story of Japan by following on immediately with pages 64–65, Japan and the League.

Discussion point: Does Japan have similar problems today? If not, why not?

5 Keeping the peace

The League of Nations (pages 48–51)

This unit first sets out the aims, organisation, powers, strengths and weaknesses of the League. Then an exercise asks students to assess the likely success of the League in dealing with five problems. Problems 1–3 occurred in the 1920s and the outcomes follow on page 53. Problems 4 and 5 are covered on pages 64–68.

Worksheets 18 and 19 help students record key information about the League.

Discussion point: What similar organisation tries to keep the peace today? Does it have similar strengths and weaknesses?

The work of the League in the 1920s (pages 52–55)

Students are asked to decide if the League was successful in dealing with problems in the 1920s.

Worksheet 20 is a framework for recording the actions of the League in the 1920s.

Discussion point: Are there similar problems in the world today?

The Great Depression – Causes and consequences (pages 56–59)

The causes of the Depression are dealt with briefly as these pages concentrate on the impact of the Depression and how it affected international relations. On page 58 students are asked to match seven problems to seven countries; this requires some recall. For ease of reference: Problem 1 is Japan, 2 is the USA, 3 is the USSR, 4 is Germany, 5 is France, 6 is Britain and 7 is Italy.

The Depression can prove to be a learning trouble spot in that students often confuse it with hyperinflation in Germany in 1923.

Question 5: The other catastrophes were the two World Wars.

Discussion point: Trade depressions occur today, do countries react in similar ways today? If not, why not?

Germany in the Depression (pages 60–63)

This unit concentrates first on how the Depression helped Hitler to power and then on Nazi beliefs. It is a key unit for showing the links between the economic and political legacy of Versailles, the causes and consequences of the Depression, Nazi aims and the threat to world peace.

Source **D** shows a few of the many parties in Weimar Germany with the Nazis a match for them all. These parties included: DNVP – Nationalists, extreme right-wing; Zentrum – Centre Party; SDP – Social Democrats; KPD – Communists; BVP – Bavarian People's Party; DVP – German People's Party, right-wing liberal.

Source **E** warns vote 'National Socialist or the sacrifices (of the war) were all in vain'.

Discussion point: Neo-Nazism in Germany today?

6 The League of Nations in the 1930s

Japan and the League (pages 64–65)

The interesting question here is how important for the future of the League was the failure in Manchuria. Source **E** is a German cartoon from *Simplicissimus* January 1933, showing the various 'children' of the League in the charge of a senile League, and Japan attacking China. If you are following the story of Japan and China straight through it continues on pages 90–94, Japan invades China 1937–39 and The spread of war 1939–41.

Discussion point: Which is more powerful today – China or Japan?

Abyssinia and the League (pages 66–68)

Before looking at the events and consequences, students are presented with the problem of saving Abyssinia and avoiding alienation with Italy. Students choose a policy and find out the consequences. Examination of all the policies, results and consequences is advisable. Policy 5 is the Hoare-Laval Pact. Sources **C** and **D** are from *Punch*.

Worksheet 21 is a cloze exercise.

Discussion point: Italy was desperate for an empire. Why do the European countries not have empires today?

The League and disarmament (page 69)

This page completes the story of disarmament which began on page 10 with the arms race before the First World War, continuing on page 18 with the disarmament of Germany at Versailles; pages 24–25 the other Peace Treaties; page 32 the Washington Conference and Rapallo Treaty; pages 34–35 France building the Maginot Line and page 55 the League and disarmament.

Discussion point: Is disarmament a possibility today?

The failure of the League (pages 70–71)

Some students may find it difficult to appreciate that countries usually act out of self-interest rather than for the common good. Do Sources **A** and **B** show that Baldwin was far-sighted, or a Prime Minister who had allowed Britain's defences seriously to deteriorate and was now worried, or one who was finding excuses not to help save Abyssinia?

Discussion point: Do countries act out of self-interest today? Give examples.

7 Steps to war 1933–39

Step 1? 1933–35 (pages 72–73)

The events of 1933–39 provide a lengthy story, therefore, to help students this section contains an ongoing activity in which they make six decisions advising Britain and France how to respond to aggression. Worksheet 22 provides a framework to organise these decisions. Because of these decisions this section does not contain teaching ideas.

Another ongoing activity begins with Question 4 which asks students to write a report on the likelihood of war and update it. Worksheet 23 provides a summary of events 1933–39 with spaces to be filled – to help students the answers could be listed in random order on the board: Anschluss, appeasement, France x 3, Stresa, two, Germany, Poland x 3, Italy x 3, Spanish, Locarno, Britain, Lebensraum, Abyssinia, Schuschnigg, Saar, Versailles, Reich, Anglo-German Naval, Rhineland, Sudeten, Neville Chamberlain, Nazi-Soviet, Munich, 1 September, Stalin.

Step 2? The Rhineland 1936 (pages 74–75)

This asks students to study the factors considered by Britain and France on how to react and then take Decision 2. Question 5 asks for a second entry in the report on the likelihood of war. The number of points on these pages make for a difficult unit.

Step 3? Spain and Austria 1936–38 (pages 76–77)

Students are faced with Decision 3 on Austria and a further entry in the report (Question 4).

Step 4? Czechoslovakia 1938 (pages 78–81)

This presents students with Decision 4 and a further entry in the report (Question 5). The exercise on page 81 asks students to make a number of decisions from the point of view of different people in March 1939. These decisions require students to refer to previous pages and provide an opportunity to take stock at a crucial stage in events. Worksheet 24 is a map exercise on how the Munich Agreement weakened Czechoslovakia.
Discussion point: Does Germany dominate Europe today?

Appeasement 1938 (pages 82–83)

Students are presented with the cases for and against appeasement and then asked if appeasement appeared sensible. Some reasons for differing interpretation are given.

It may be worth first looking again at pages 36–37 which explain why Britain followed a policy of appeasement in the 1920s and 1930s. The aim of Worksheet 25 is to help students compare the cases for and against appeasement.
Teaching idea: Use the cases for and against to write newspaper front pages to go with the differing interpretations in Sources **A** and **B**.

8 The final steps to war

The Nazi-Soviet Pact (pages 84–87)

This emphasises the choices faced by Chamberlain and Stalin:
1) Should Britain ally with Poland or Russia? Students meet this dilemma in Decision 5 – students should respond after having read the first paragraph of Decision 5.
2) Should Russia ally with Germany or with Britain and France?

3) Should Britain accept Hitler's offer to leave the British Empire alone or go to war over Poland. Students meet this dilemma in Decision 6.

The seven reasons why Stalin signed a treaty with Hitler in 'Events' are: 1. The six weeks it took Britain to reply. 2. The Japanese attack. 3. No senior British people were sent to negotiate. 4. The length of the Battle of Nomonhan. 5. The Polish refusal to allow Russian troops to cross Poland. 6. The personal approach by Hitler and Ribbentrop. 7. The German offer of Russian control of parts of Eastern Europe. The state of the British and French armies is another reason given in Choice two. Worksheet 26 is a framework for recording information on the Nazi-Soviet Pact.
Source **E** is a British cartoon dated 2 October 1939. Page 87 asks students to compare the causes of the two World Wars. You may prefer to attempt this difficult task after studying pages 88–89. Worksheet 28 is to help with this task.
Discussion point: Do we learn from our past mistakes? Have we learnt any lessons from History since 1939?

The causes of war – Interpretations (pages 88–89)

These pages pull together much of the work done so far and ask students to prioritise the causes of war. Worksheet 27 is a copy of Source **A**. Students may well need more space than that provided to complete the sentence in the centre box. Source **A** can also be used as a revision exercise with students using the index and contents page to find and revise each cause. Source **B** appeared on 11 April, immediately after the Easter holiday. It compares the litter commonly produced after such a holiday with the litter of international agreements since Munich: Peace is trying to clear up the mess of the broken pacts, treaties and agreements but is under a heavy burden. The most recent breach was the Italian invasion of Albania on 7 April which broke the 'Anglo-Italian Pact' of November 1938.
Teaching ideas:
- Source **A** could be the basis for group work in which groups use it to help argue in support of one of the interpretations.
- Enlarge two copies of Source **A** and cut out the causes as separate cards. Shuffle the cards and deal them face down to the class. Students with the same cards form pairs and then have one minute to argue why their cause is the most important; alternatively they research it and explain to the class how it contributed to causing the war.
- A whole class approach is to see if agreement can be reached in eliminating the least important causes.
Discussion point: Which events do students have differing interpretations about? (For example, a football match.)

9 The world at war 1937–41

Japan invades China 1937–39 (pages 90–91)

The explicit sources in this unit aim to help students remember that the war began in East Asia in 1937 and show some of the brutality of the Japanese attack.

Discussion point: Why was the 'Rape of Nanking (Nanjing)' not mentioned in Japanese textbooks until recently. How might this affect interpretations of the causes of war held by the Japanese?

The spread of war 1939–41 (pages 92–95)

This unit explains how Russia, the USA and Japan became involved in the war, in particular the attack on Pearl Harbor. To help with Question 5 students can refer to their work on Source **A** on page 88 and the list in Question 4, page 95.

Discussion point: Do students know the names of the leaders of the most powerful countries today? Do you think another world war is likely today?

Worksheets 29–32 ask students to work on developments over a period of time.

Worksheet 29 asks students to consider when the threat to world peace became more serious between 1919–39.

Worksheet 30 covers Russia's relations with other countries 1919–41.

Worksheet 31 covers the USA and international relations 1914–41.

Worksheet 32 covers Japan and international relations 1919–1941.

Worksheet 33 asks students to use the index in their book to place events between 1919–1941 in sequence and make links between the two World Wars.

Worksheet 34 is an extension exercise looking at Hitler's responsibility for the war (a MEG Focus point).

GCSE syllabus matching guide

MEG Syllabus B: Modern World
International Relations, 1919–c.1989
This is a compulsory core paper. Content is explained through a number of Key Questions and Focus Points. Specified content is also given. The pupils' book covers the first three Key Questions.

Syllabus content	Pupils' book content	Pupils' book page no.
1 Were the Peace Treaties of 1919–23 fair?		
Specified content		
The Peace Treaties of 1919–23 (Versailles, St. Germain, Trianon, Neuilly, Sevres and Lausanne)	The Treaty of Versailles – The terms The other Peace Treaties	18–19 24–25
The roles of individuals such as Wilson, Clemenceau and Lloyd George in the peacemaking process	The Treaty of Versailles – The peacemakers	16–17
The impact of the treaties on the defeated countries	The Treaty of Versailles – The terms Consequences and future problems	18–19 26–29
Contemporary opinions about the treaties	Views on the Treaty of Versailles War debts and reparations Justifying the Treaty of Versailles The USA and isolationism	20–21 30–31 22–23 38–39
2 To what extent was the League of Nations a success?		
Specified content		
Strengths and weaknesses in its structure	The League of Nations	48–51
Successes and failures in peace-keeping during the 1920s	The work of the League in the 1920s Treaties and pacts in the 1920s	52–55 32–33
The impact of the World Depression on the work of the League after 1929	The Great Depression – Causes and consequences	56–59
The failures of the League during the 1930s, including Manchuria and Abyssinia	Japan and the League Abyssinia and the League The League and disarmament The failure of the League	64–65 66–68 69 70–71
3 Why had international peace collapsed by 1939?		
The collapse of international order in the 1930s	Units 6–9	64–95
The increasing militarism of Germany, Italy and Japan	Germany in the Depression Mussolini and Fascist Italy Abyssinia and the League Japan's problems Japan invades China 1937–39 The spread of war 1939–41	60–63 44–45 66–68 46–47 90–91 92–95
Hitler's foreign policy to 1939	Step 1? 1933–35 Step 2? The Rhineland 1936 Step 3? Spain and Austria 1936–38 Step 4? Czechoslovakia 1938	72–73 74–75 76–77 78–81
Appeasement and the outbreak of war in 1939	Appeasement 1938 The Nazi-Soviet Pact The causes of war – Interpretations	82–83 84–87 88–89

Many of the Focus Points in the MEG syllabus are also directly addressed by the Key Questions at the beginning of each unit, for example:

MEG Syllabus	Pupils' book Key Question	Pupils' book page no.
1 Were the Peace Treaties of 1919–23 fair?		
Focus points:		
What were the motives and aims of the Big Three at Versailles?	What were the aims of the Peacemakers?	16–17
Why did all of the victors not get everything they wanted?	Did the peacemakers get the terms they wanted?	18–19
What was the immediate impact of the Peace Treaty on Germany?	What problems did Germany face?	40–41
Could the treaties be justified at the time?	Was the Treaty of Versailles justified at the time?	22–23

SEG Syllabus B: Modern World

Peace to war, 1919–39

This is a study unit for examination in Paper 2

Syllabus content	Pupils' book content	Pupils' book page no.
The Paris peace settlement of 1919–20		
The main personalities – Wilson, Clemenceau, Lloyd George – and their attitudes towards the defeated countries	The Treaty of Versailles – The peacemakers	16–17
The main terms of the Treaty of Versailles	The Treaty of Versailles – The terms	18–19
The other treaties and the main territorial changes	The other Peace treaties	24–25
Problems associated with the peace settlement		
Reasons for resentment and bitterness in Germany	Views on the Treaty of Versailles Justifying the Treaty of Versailles	20–21 22–23
The question of reparations and their revision in 1923–24 and 1929 (the Dawes and Young Plans)	War debts and reparations	30–31
The failure of the League of Nations		
The powers, membership and peace-keeping role of the League	The League of Nations The work of the League in the 1920s	48–51 52–55
Japanese expansion into Manchuria and China, the Italian conquest of Abyssinia, and the response of the League to these events	Japan and the League Abyssinia and the League	64–65 66–68
The reasons for and the implications of the League's failure	The failure of the League	70–71
German actions and expansion		
Violations of the Treaty of Versailles, 1934–38 – rearmament, conscription, reoccupation of the Rhineland, Austria	Step 1? 1933–35 Step 2? The Rhineland 1936 Step 3? Spain and Austria 1936–38	72–73 74–75 76–77
The role of Chamberlain; appeasement	Britain and the world 1919–33	36–37

and the reasons for it	Appeasement 1938	82–83
The Sudetenland, 1938; March 1939; the invasion of Poland	Step 4? Czechoslovakia 1938	78–81
The changing attitudes of Britain, France and the Soviet Union, 1938–39	The Nazi-Soviet Pact	84–87
The role of Hitler	The causes of war – Interpretations	88–89

NEAB Syllabus B: Modern World

Origins of conflict – the events leading to the Second World War 1919–39.

This is unit 4 of the Paper 1 theme: Conflict in the Modern World.

Syllabus content	Pupils' book content	Pupils' book page no.
4.1 How successful was Hitler in challenging and exploiting the Versailles Treaty?		
Versailles Treaty 1919: Hitler's aims and expansionist policies: the Saar, Rhineland, Austria. The growth of the armed forces	The Treaty of Versailles – The peacemakers	16–17
	The Treaty of Versailles – The terms	18–19
	Germany in the Depression	60–63
	Step 1? 1933–35	72–73
	Step 2? The Rhineland 1936	74–75
	Step 3? Spain and Austria 1936–38	76–77
4.2 Why did appeasement fail to prevent the outbreak of war in 1939?		
Chamberlain and appeasement: Czechoslovakia	Step 4? Czechoslovakia 1938	78–81
	Appeasement 1938	82–83
The role of the USSR: Munich and the Nazi-Soviet Pact	The Nazi-Soviet Pact	84–87
Poland and the outbreak of war	The Nazi-Soviet Pact	84–87

Theme 3: Aspects of the Twentieth-century (Coursework or Paper 3)

Aspect c) in this theme is International Co-operation. *International Relations 1919–39* covers Units 1 and 2 of this aspect.

Syllabus content	Pupils' book content	Pupils' book page no.
Unit 1: The League of Nations		
1.1 The key features of the League	The League of Nations	48–51
1.2 The main successes of the League	The work of the League in the 1920s	52–55
Unit 2: Manchuria & Abyssinia case studies		
Why did the League fail in handling the crisis in Manchuria?	Japan and the League	64–65
Why did the League fail in handling the crisis in Abyssinia?	Abyssinia and the League	66–68
	The failure of the League	70–71

EDEXCEL Syllabus A: Modern European and World History

International Relations 1919–39 can be useful for parts of the following studies:
Depth Study B2 contains: The defeat of Germany and the Peace Settlement.
Depth Study B5 contains: Appeasement, 1938–9: the role of Chamberlain; the outbreak of the Second World War.

EDEXCEL Syllabus D: Schools History Project

International Relations 1919–39 provides material suitable for Coursework Unit C2 – International Study. This concentrates on the interaction of causes and effects and the importance of the role played by individuals, groups and nations.

Overview

Why did world peace after 1919 last only to 1939?

This chart is a copy of Source **B** on page 5 of the pupils' book. It helps to give you an overview of international relations between 1919–39. Use the page numbers which appear in some of the boxes to find examples of particular problems. You can do this either as a way of introducing yourself to this book or at a later stage as a revision exercise.

Events leading up to the Second World War

FIRST WORLD WAR 1914–18

Led to the Peace Treaties, e.g. p.16

helped cause

helped cause

the League of Nations (to help solve international problems) e.g. p.53

new small countries made up of different national groups, e.g. p.24

most Germans found the terms unacceptable, e.g. p.20

the Russian Revolution 1917

poverty, damage to trade and the economy of the world, e.g. p.29

the League failed – perhaps this encouraged countries to go to war, e.g. p.71

these small countries could not defend themselves, e.g. p.84

Hitler's promise to tear up the Treaty of Versailles helped him to gain power

a different political system which frightened many other countries, their feelings ranged from suspicion to fear and to hatred

helped cause the Great Depression, e.g. p.56

Soviet Russia did not trust capitalist countries and they did not trust Soviet Russia, e.g. p.85

the Depression helped Hitler rise to power and encouraged Japanese aggression, e.g. p.58

SECOND WORLD WAR 1939–45

2 *International relations 1919–41*

What were the major events in international relations 1919–41?

This is the timeline (Source **B)** on pages 4–5 of the pupils' book.

Revolution in Russia p.6

US isolation begins p.38

Mussolini comes to power in Italy p.44

US stock market crashes p.56

Japan's invasion of China begins p.64

Hitler comes to power p.60

German troops reoccupy the Rhineland p.74
Spanish Civil War begins p.76

Japan controls most of Eastern China p.90
Germany takes control of parts of Czechoslovakia p.78

Germany invades Poland and the Second World War begins p.86

Germany attacks Russia p.92
Japan attacks US base at Pearl Harbor p.94

1914

1917

1918

1919

1920

1922

1929

1931

1934

1936

1938

1939

1941

World Economic Depression

WAR

Peace Treaties

Work of the League of Nations Mostly successes

Mostly failures

Collapse of International Peace

Steps to war in Europe and the Far East

WAR IN EUROPE – WORLD WAR

Key History for GCSE: International Relations 1919–39 – Teacher's Guide © Stanley Thornes (Publishers) Ltd. 1998

3 Governments

What types of governments were there in post-war Europe?

To show the political nature of different governments and any changes that took place colour the column for each country using the key. For example Germany will change colour in 1934. Page 8 and the following additional information will help you.

Russia was communist from 1917.
Germany was a democracy 1919–34.
Spain was a democracy 1931–36 and at civil war 1936–39 (communist vs. republicans).
Japan was nationalist.
China was nationalist 1911–1927 and at civil war (communist vs. nationalist).

Democratic = blue
Communist = red
Fascist   = green
Nationalist = yellow

Political System	Europe						Outside Europe		
	Britain	France	Russia/ USSR	Germany	Italy	Spain	USA	China	Japan
1911									
1914									
1917									
1919									
1927									
1931									
1934									
1936									
1939									

4 *Solving the causes of the war*

How would you solve the problems which caused the war?

This worksheet provides a framework for your solutions to the problems on pages 10–11. It also provides space for the best idea in the class – if you can agree.

Problems	Ideas on how to avoid each problem	
	My idea	**The best idea in the class**
1 The rise of Germany		
2 The Arms Race		
3 Problems in the Austro-Hungarian Empire		
4 The problem of Empire		
5 The Alliance System		

5 The Peacemakers

What were the aims of the peacemakers?

This worksheet is to help you organise your responses to the questions 1–7 on page 16. Write a brief answer in the column of each leader. For example the first two questions for Clemenceau have been answered. In the final column enter a ✓ if all three leaders agree, or a ✗ if they do not agree.

	Lloyd George Britain	Clemenceau France	Wilson USA	Do all three leaders agree?
1 Who started the war?		Germany		
2 Should the Kaiser be put on trial?		Yes		
3 Should Germany pay reparations? How much?				
4 Should Germany keep any armed forces? How many?				
5 What should happen to Germany's colonies?				
6 Should Germany and Austria be allowed to unite?				
7 Germany's borders. Which country should control the following areas of Germany?				
a) Alsace-Lorraine				
b) The Saar				
c) Eupen/Malmedy				
d) The Rhineland				
e) Schleswig				
f) West Prussia				
g) Posen and Thorn				
h) Danzig				
i) Allenstein/Marienwerder				
j) Upper Silesia				
k) Memel				

6 The reshaping of Europe at Versailles

What territory did Germany lose at Versailles?

This is a copy of Source **B** on page 17. Colour in the map according to the key.
You will first need to read pages 18–19 and use Source **A** on page 18 to find
out what happened to each area.

Key
Land lost by Germany = Red
Areas controlled by the League of Nations = Yellow
Demilitarised area = Shaded purple

1 Alsace-Lorraine
Important industrial area; claimed by France (had
been French until 1870).
2 Saar
Large coalfields; claimed by France but with a German
population.
3 Eupen/Malmedy
Important coal and iron resources; claimed by
Belgium (Belgium was neutral in 1914 and suffered
badly when Germany invaded).
4 Rhineland
Claimed by France for protection, but had a German
population.
5 Schleswig
Population a mixture of Germans (more in the South)
and Danes (more in the North). Claimed by Denmark
but German since the 1860s.

6 West Prussia
7 Posen and Thorn
German-speaking areas, claimed by Poland. Essential
to give Poland access to the sea, but this would
separate East Prussia from the rest of Germany.
8 Danzig
An important port; claimed by Poland but with a
German-speaking population.
9 Allenstein/Marienwerder
10 Upper Silesia
Mixed population of Germans and Poles.
11 Memel
Between Lithuania and East Prussia, claimed by
Lithuania.

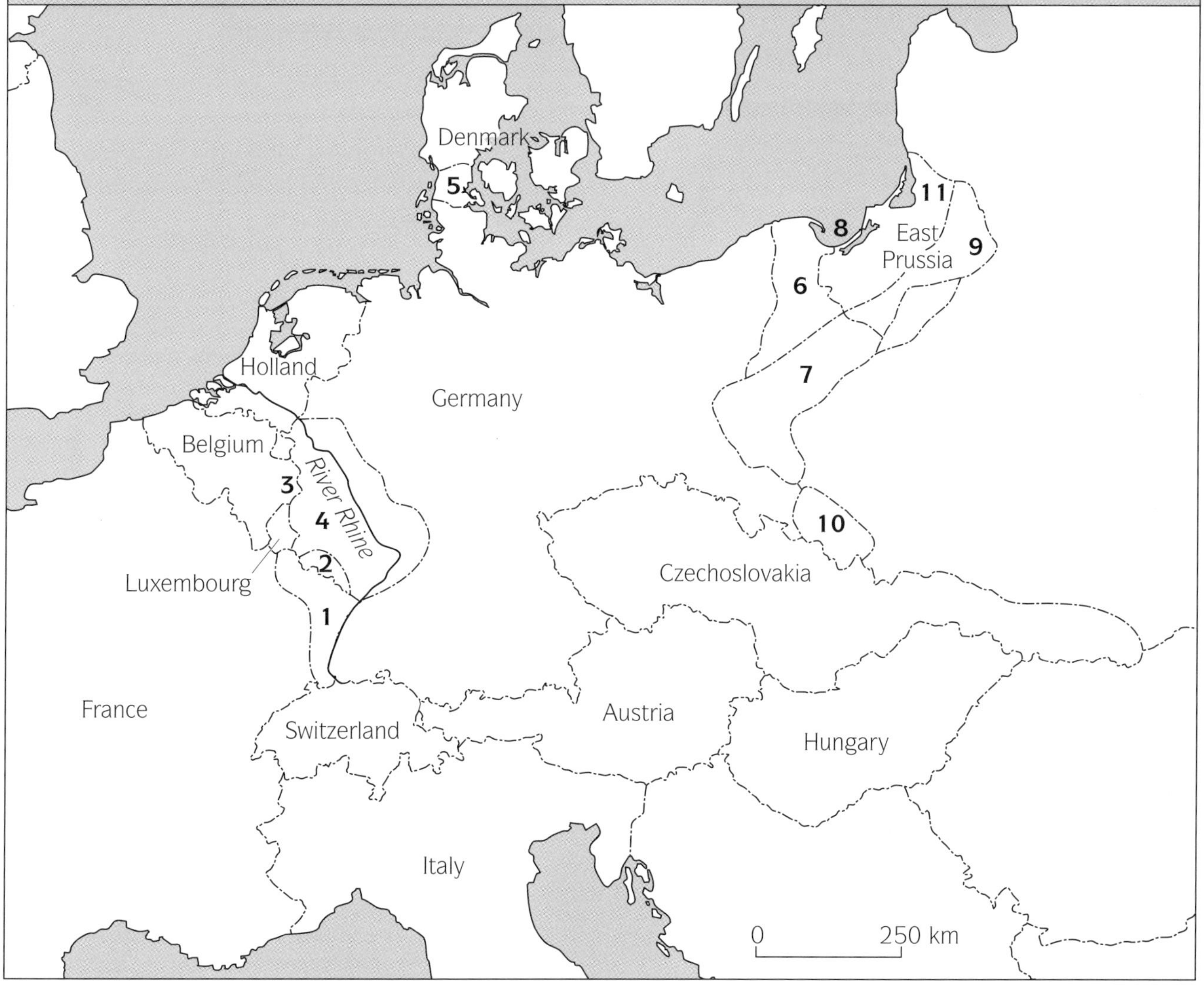

[Map of central Europe showing Germany and surrounding countries: Denmark, Holland, Belgium, Luxembourg, France, Switzerland, Italy, Austria, Hungary, Czechoslovakia, East Prussia. Numbered areas 1–11 marked on the map, with the River Rhine labelled. Scale: 0 – 250 km]

7 The Treaty of Versailles – The views of historians

What do historians think of the Versailles Treaty?

Below are the views of different historians on the Treaty. Read them carefully.

1
…the settlement that emerged was a creditable achievement. The fact that it did not survive the 1920s intact stemmed… not so much from the terms of the peace treaties themselves, but from the reluctance of political leaders of the inter-war period to enforce them.

Ruth Henig

2
The Versailles Treaty may not have been grossly unfair given the damage that Germany had inflicted on its rivals… but it was unwise.

Paul Bookbinder

3
Germany fought specifically in the Second World War to remove the verdict of the first and to destroy the settlement which followed it.

A J P Taylor

4
Intrinsically there was nothing wrong with the Treaty of Versailles. It was neither unjust nor unworkable. The only trouble with it was that the statesman who drafted it never attempted to enforce more of its territorial provisions.

Delme

5
Severe though the terms were, in some respects they were less so than might have been expected.

E Kolb

6
Few would dispute that, given the remarkable range of conditions and factors bearing on the task of peacemaking in war-torn Europe, the Treaty of Versailles was a remarkable achievement.

J W Hiden

7
To the discerning it was clear from the beginning that the Versailles settlement would last as long as the victorious powers were in a position to enforce it on a bitterly resentful people.

Carr

1 Use the points made by the historians to make **a)** a list of points defending the Treaty of Versailles, and **b)** a list of points criticising the Treaty.

2 Which of the views suggest that the Treaty helped cause the Second World War?

3 Which of the words opposite do you think apply to the Treaty of Versailles?

unwise   reasonable   difficult

severe   unworkable   lenient

unfair   stupid   creditable

8 Justifying the Treaty of Versailles (1)

Was the Treaty of Versailles justified?

This worksheet is a copy of the chart on page 23 of the pupils' book with space to add your reasons.

Aims	Was the aim reasonable? Yes/No Reasons	Terms	Was the term a fair way of achieving the aim? Yes/No Reasons
1a) Germany to be made solely responsible for the war. **b)** Germany should pay for the damage.		'War Guilt' Clause. Reparations (later fixed at £6,600,000,000).	
2 Germany must never be able to start another war.		German army only 100,000 men, small navy, no tanks, war planes or submarines.	
3 People should have the right to national self-determination.		Rhineland to be demilitarised. Germany to lose areas containing other nationals (see chart on p.23): 1 Alsace-Lorraine 2 Eupen-Malmedy 3 Schleswig 4 West Prussia 5 Posen and Thorn 6 Danzig 7 Allenstein/ Marienwerder 8 Upper Silesia 9 Memel	

9 *Justifying the Treaty of Versailles (2)*

Did you decide that the Treaty of Versailles was justified? If you did, were you influenced by who you think was responsible for causing the war? The War Guilt Clause blamed Germany and so did most British people in 1919, and so do most British people today. The reasons are clear:

Account 1

1 Germany was threatening British naval supremacy. Britain needed a strong navy to protect her empire. Germany only had a small empire. In 1905 and 1911 Germany tried to interfere in the French Empire in North Africa. So Germany could not be trusted.

2 When the heir to the Austro-Hungarian throne was assassinated by a Serbian it was Germany that encouraged Austria-Hungary to attack Serbia and thus trigger the Alliance System which plunged Europe into war.

3 It was Germany who declared war on Russia and France. It was Germany who invaded Belgium in order to attack France. Britain had guaranteed Belgium neutrality back in 1839 and had no choice but to honour its agreement and stand by Belgium.

But is this account misleading? What if it omits certain important information? After all they do say that the victors write history to justify their actions. What if Britain wanted war for its own reasons? Would this affect your decision on whether the Treaty of Versailles was justified? Consider the following account.

Account 2

Britain's main aim was to keep a balance of power in Europe between Germany and France. Britain was worried that when Germany defeated France in 1870 Germany would dominate Europe. Germany wanted closer relations with Britain for the benefit of Europe, but Britain did not want this. For example during quarrels between Europe and the USA in 1898 and 1902 it was Germany who wanted to stand firm against the USA, but Britain would not.

Germany decided to build up her own navy to enable her to act on her own and defend her new overseas colonies. Britain saw this as a threat to her communications with her own empire, and thus its defence. So Britain stepped up her naval building programme by building larger ships called 'super dreadnoughts' with 12 inch guns. German warships only had 10 inch guns and so were obsolete. They also had to start building larger ships.

The growth of the German navy caused a change in mood amongst the British public. Until 1885 they had feared Russia and France, indeed the British public had demanded plans for a cross

Channel tunnel be abandoned. Then this fear switched to a fear of Germany. It was encouraged by the printing of popular invasion stories. Perhaps the most important of these was published in 1903 – *The Riddle of the Sands* by Erskine Childers.

Below is an extract from this book. The hero, Carruthers, is on a sailing holiday with a friend along the coast of Germany. They become suspicious of the actions of the local officials and discover a secret plan.

> An interesting document, somewhat damaged by fire, lies on my study table.
>
> It is a copy of a confidential memorandum to the German Government embodying a scheme for the invasion of England by Germany. The fact that it was taken by Carruthers from the stove of the villa at Norderney, leaves no doubt as to its authorship. I propose to give an outline of its contents… to dispatch an army of infantry with the lightest type of field-guns in big sea-going lighters (barges), towed by powerful but shallow-draught tugs, under escort of a powerful squadron of warships; and to fling the flotilla, at high tide, if possible, straight upon the shore of England.

In this book Germany was shown as devious and lacking in the British sense of fair play. Other books told of secret German armies, weapons and plans to invade Britain and of secret German agents in Britain.

In 1911 Britain reacted strongly against German attempts to extend her empire. The naval race between the two countries pushed Europe into two armed camps. To lessen the threat to her empire Britain signed 'Ententes' with France in 1904 and Russia in 1907. When Germany invaded Belgium in 1914 Britain believed it could not allow Germany to gain control of the continental side of the Channel as this was a threat to the British Navy's use of the Channel. Also British honour was at stake to stand by Belgium.

Both of these accounts are rather one sided and both ignore other important events and factors. But do you now believe all the blame for causing the war should be put on Germany? The War Guilt Clause put all the blame on Germany and this was how the 'Big Three' justified the terms forced on Germany.

Look again at your decisions on page 23 of the pupils' book. Would you change any of your decisions?

10 *The other Peace Treaties*

How were the other defeated countries treated?

This map is a copy of Source **B** on page 24 of the pupils' book. Complete the map by using the key in the book to show the land lost by Austria, Hungary and Bulgaria.

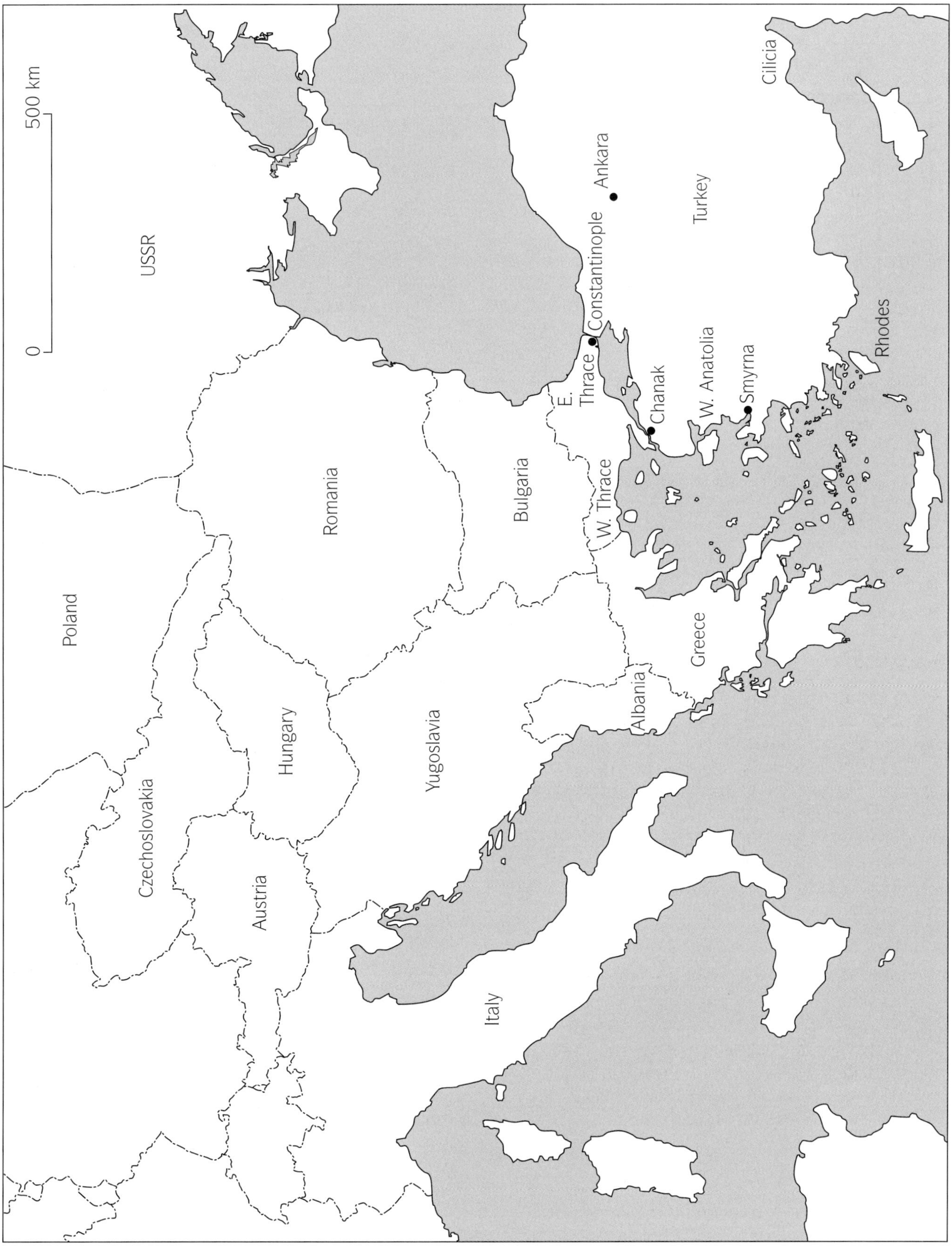

500 km
0
USSR
Poland
Czechoslovakia
Austria
Hungary
Romania
Yugoslavia
Bulgaria
Italy
Albania
Greece
W. Thrace
E. Thrace
Constantinople
Ankara
Turkey
Chanak
W. Anatolia
Smyrna
Rhodes
Cilicia

Future trouble spots?

What future trouble spots were left by the Treaty of Versailles?

This map of Europe shows a number of possible future trouble spots. Match seven of these spots with the seven people in Source **F** on page 28 of the pupils' book and briefly explain why each was a possible trouble spot. For the eighth trouble spot take a look ahead and find out what happened on page 74 of the pupils' book.

Europe in 1919

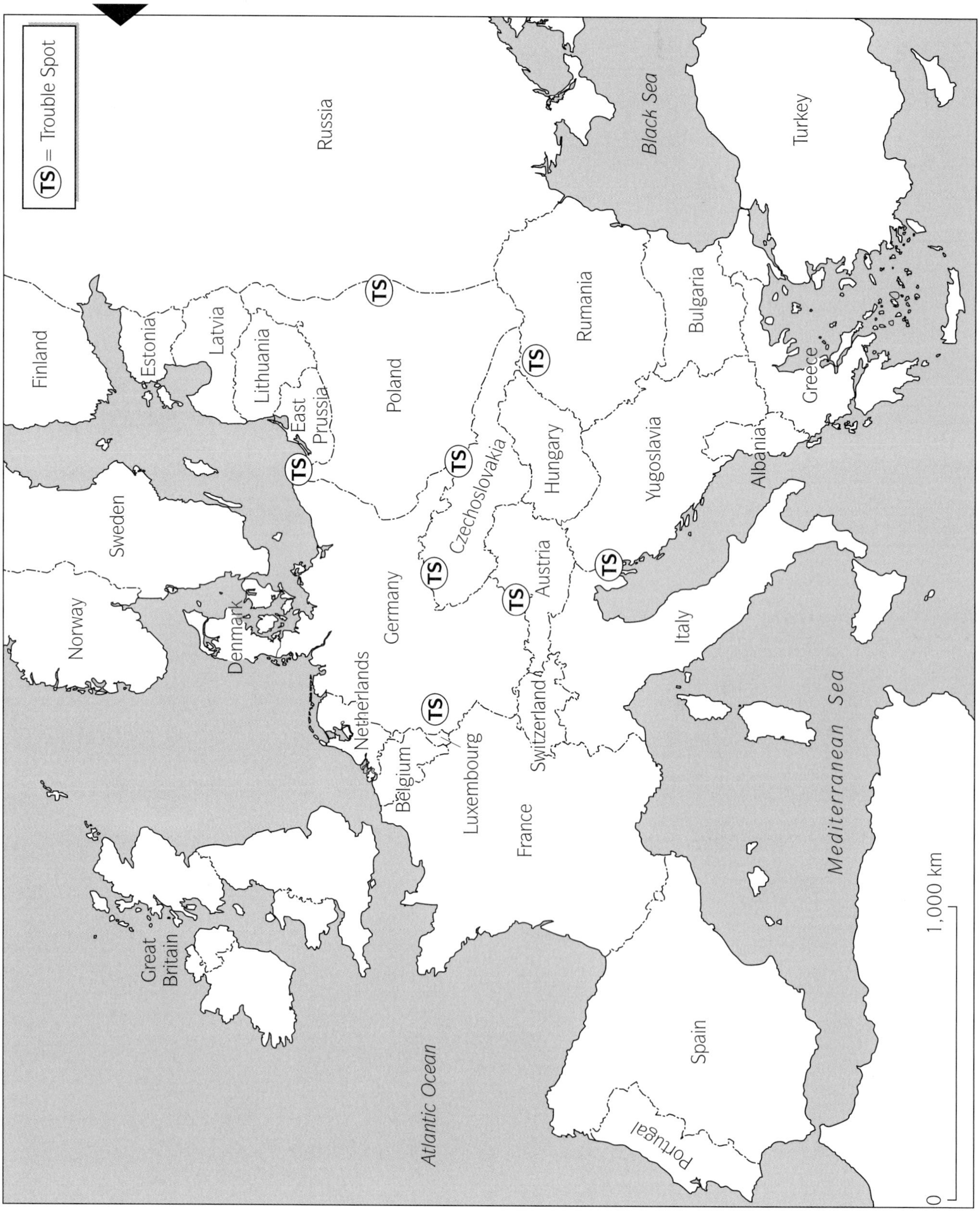

(TS) = Trouble Spot

[Map of Europe in 1919, showing countries including Finland, Sweden, Norway, Russia, Estonia, Latvia, Lithuania, East Prussia, Poland, Denmark, Netherlands, Belgium, Luxembourg, Germany, Czechoslovakia, Hungary, Austria, Switzerland, France, Great Britain, Spain, Portugal, Italy, Rumania, Yugoslavia, Bulgaria, Albania, Greece, Turkey, with Atlantic Ocean, Black Sea, Mediterranean Sea labelled. Trouble Spots (TS) marked at various locations. Scale: 1,000 km]

12 War debts and reparations

How did war debts and reparations affect international relations?

This worksheet is designed to help you check whether you understand the material covered on pages 30–31 of the pupils' book.

1 Match the word or phrase on the left with the correct definition on the right.

Reparations	An attempt by the French and Belgians to enforce payment of reparations.
Dawes Plan	The compensation to be paid for the damage caused in the war.
Stresemann	A plan in 1924 to scale down reparation payments and to loan money to Germany.
Occupation of the Ruhr	A plan in 1929 to reduce reparation payments due from Germany.
Young Plan	The refusal of German workers to work with the invading armies.
Passive resistance	The German Chancellor and later Foreign Minister who led Germany to recovery after the French occupation of the Ruhr.

2 Now write a short paragraph explaining how the words and phrases on the left are linked, i.e. how one led to another. (They are not in the correct order.)

13 Treaties and pacts in the 1920s

What treaties and pacts were signed in the 1920s?

Complete the wordsearch below. The answers to the clues can be found on pages 32–33 of the pupils' book. The answers in the grid can read forwards, backwards, up, down or diagonally. The answer to the first clue has been found for you.

Clues

1 The aim of the Washington Naval Conference.
2 The Washington Conference was concerned about this part of the world.
3 This country had one of the largest navies allowed by the Washington Treaties.
4 This country had one of the smaller navies allowed.
5 Germany and Russia signed this treaty of co-operation.
6 This was one of the armoured vehicles Germany tested in Russia forbidden under the Treaty of Versailles.
7 The aim of the Locarno Pact was to make this continent a safer place.
8 This country agreed its borders were fixed at Locarno.
9 It was agreed at Locarno that this area was to remain demilitarised.
10 This country was promised protection by France at Locarno.
11 At Locarno this country agreed to join the League of Nations.
12 The Kellogg-Briand Pact renounced the use of what?
13 Soon after signing the Kellogg-Briand Pact this country broke its promise.
14 Of all the pacts and treaties this was the one which people put most hope in.

R	A	P	A	L	L	O	C	L	R	S	P	B	O	J
M	R	E	H	W	Q	L	K	D	H	L	W	T	A	K
G	E	R	M	A	N	Y	U	D	I	C	I	P	N	T
H	A	V	Z	R	M	L	G	R	N	D	A	S	C	N
B	W	F	M	F	C	A	L	O	E	N	O	C	K	E
C	P	A	E	A	G	T	Q	D	L	P	S	B	O	M
I	I	P	E	R	M	I	T	G	A	A	U	R	B	A
E	Y	U	O	E	L	F	Y	E	N	J	P	U	A	M
K	N	A	T	E	U	S	E	P	D	X	A	S	S	R
H	C	G	H	B	K	E	R	H	J	R	S	I	N	A
N	D	O	V	F	B	P	A	C	I	F	I	C	X	S
L	O	C	A	R	N	O	J	A	P	A	R	N	J	I
M	W	A	I	K	S	R	D	I	R	E	A	A	R	D
T	B	E	L	G	I	U	M	Y	O	A	L	M	Z	A
F	X	M	U	L	T	E	U	Q	D	N	A	L	O	P

14 *France searches for security*

Why was France so afraid of Germany?

What steps did France take to defend herself?

To do

How good a leader of France would you be? Use a coin to play security snakes and ladders. Heads = 1 move. Tails = 2 moves.

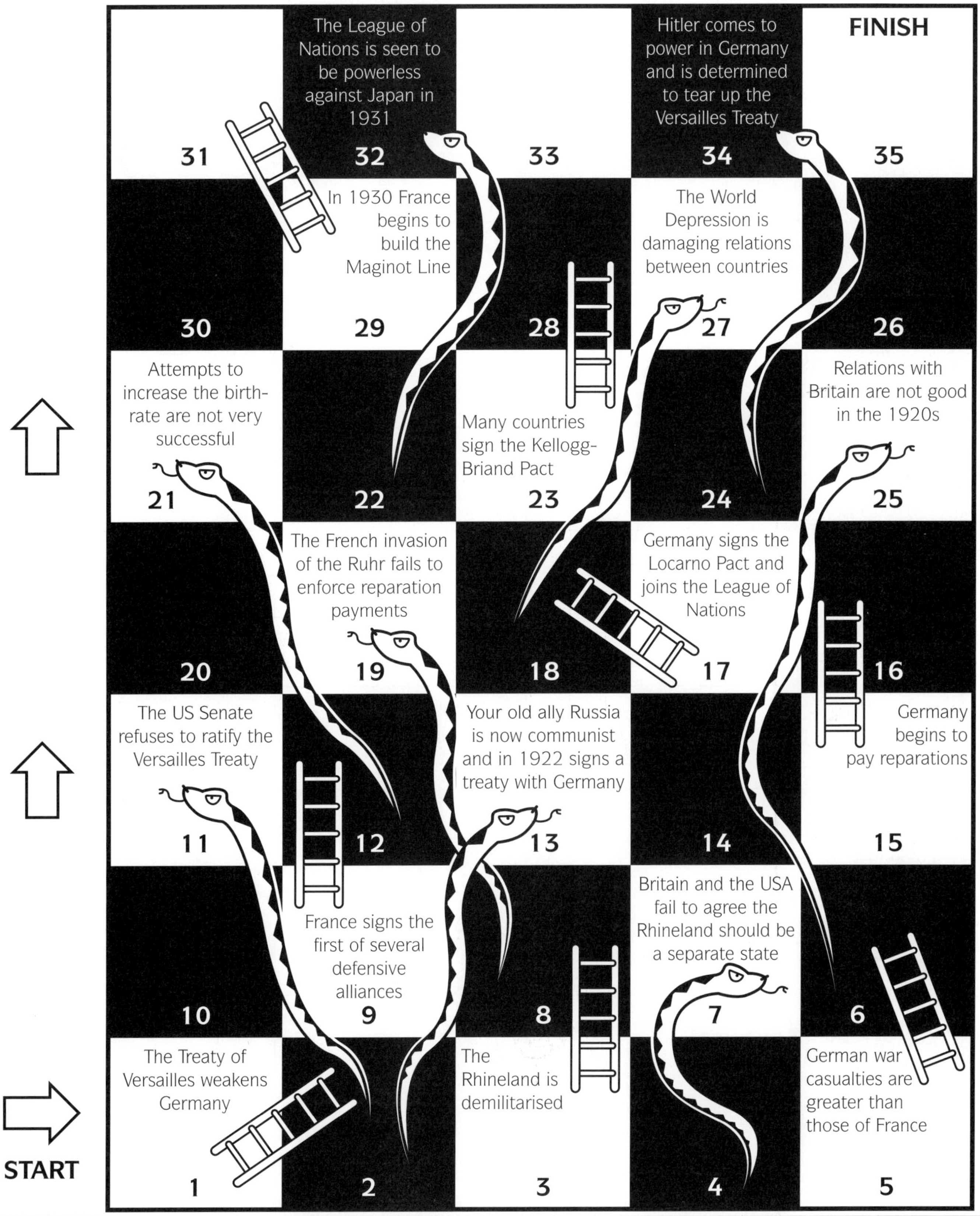

31	The League of Nations is seen to be powerless against Japan in 1931 **32**	**33**	Hitler comes to power in Germany and is determined to tear up the Versailles Treaty **34**	**FINISH** **35**
30	In 1930 France begins to build the Maginot Line **29**	**28**	The World Depression is damaging relations between countries **27**	**26**
Attempts to increase the birth-rate are not very successful **21**	**22**	Many countries sign the Kellogg-Briand Pact **23**	Germany signs the Locarno Pact and joins the League of Nations **24**	Relations with Britain are not good in the 1920s **25**
20	The French invasion of the Ruhr fails to enforce reparation payments **19**	**18**	**17**	**16**
The US Senate refuses to ratify the Versailles Treaty **11**	**12**	Your old ally Russia is now communist and in 1922 signs a treaty with Germany **13**	**14**	Germany begins to pay reparations **15**
10	France signs the first of several defensive alliances **9**	**8**	Britain and the USA fail to agree the Rhineland should be a separate state **7**	**6**
The Treaty of Versailles weakens Germany **1**	**2**	The Rhineland is demilitarised **3**	**4**	German war casualties are greater than those of France **5**

START

15 *Britain and the world 1919–33*

What policy should Britain adopt?

This worksheet helps you organise your answers to the task on pages 36–37 of the pupils' book. You are asked to decide which policy Britain should follow in the 1920s and 1930s. Complete the chart by placing a ✔ if a policy satisfies a concern or overcomes a problem, if it does not then place a ✗ instead.

Concerns	Policy 1 Disarm and rely on the League of Nations.	Policy 2 Spend to defend the Empire and enforce the Peace Treaties	Policy 3 Appeasement – avoid conflict by accepting changes to the Peace Treaties. Only fight as a last resort.
1 The British Empire			
2 The British economy			
3 The need to spend less			
4 The need to improve living standards			
5 The need for peace			
Problems			
1 The USA refuses to join the League of Nations			
2 Conscript soldiers need to be demobbed			
3 Nationalist movements in the Empire			
4 Countries unhappy with the Peace Treaties			
5 The threat of new weapons			

16 The USA and isolationism

Why did the USA reject the Treaty of Versailles and the League of Nations?

The US President, Woodrow Wilson, proposed the setting up of the League of Nations in the hope it would keep world peace. Many Americans, however, hated the idea. They had had enough of Europe's problems.

1 Join each person on the left to the correct sentence on the right.

2 Explain why each person might have been against the League of Nations.

An Austrian-American.	Most Irish-Americans wanted Ireland to be free of British rule. The statesmen at Versailles had ignored this request. British influence was too strong.
An American soldier who lost both legs in the war.	Millions of US$ were lent to the defeated powers to help them recover and pay reparations.
An American banker whose bank has been asked to loan money to Germany.	America's business is business, not peace-keeping. The League of Nations could use economic sanctions to restrict trade.
An American who believes the League of Nations will only be used to protect the interests of Britain and France.	Many Americans had been wounded and had lost relatives fighting what many believed was a war over a European quarrel.
An Irish-American who supported demands for an independent Ireland.	Most Austrian and German Americans felt the peace treaties were wrong and the USA should not have been persuaded to join Britain and France in the war.
A rich American businessman who owns a clothing factory.	Many Americans believed the USA should at all costs avoid any promises which might again involve her in Europe's problems.

What was the impact of Versailles on Germany up to 1923?

Death rather than slavery

This was the headline of the nationalist newspaper *Deutsche Zeitung*. Defeat in the war was a great shock for most Germans. They had expected to win it. The terms of the Versailles Treaty made it worse and the new Weimar Republic took the blame. The immediate impact of the Treaty on Germany can be seen in the following areas:

Revolts

In March 1920 a right-wing revolt led by Wolfgang Kapp forced the Government to flee Berlin. Kapp set up a new government but it collapsed when workers went on strike. Then in November 1923 Hitler, at the head of his small National Socialist German Workers' Party, led a poorly organised revolt in Munich. This failed when the authorities stood firm.

Reparations

These were to plague the Weimar Republic until the very end. The German government adopted a policy of trying to fulfil the terms but at the same time showing how impossible it was to pay. Trouble in paying led to France invading the Ruhr and the hyperinflation of 1923.

Hatred of Weimar politicians

Many right-wing Germans hated the politicians who had been forced to sign the Versailles Treaty. Political violence was common in Germany between 1919–23 and there were many assassinations. The most important was that of Dr Walther Rathenau the Foreign Minister. He had worked hard at trying to improve the terms at Versailles. His assassination was the 378th political murder and in 353 cases the guilty persons either escaped or were acquitted by sympathetic courts.

For each of the Germans below explain:

a) how they would be likely to react to the new democratic government;

b) their hopes and fears for the future.

1 A soldier who fought in the trenches and believed in 1918 that victory was in sight. He still has his rifle.

2 A widow who lost her husband in the war.

3 A grandmother who remembers Germany beating France in 1870.

4 A left-wing politician who is glad to see the end of the Kaiser's rule.

5 A right-wing politician who believes democracy means weak leadership.

6 A Social Democratic politician in the Government who believes Germany must look to the future, not the past.

18 The League of Nations – Organisation

How did the League work?

Use pages 48–49 of the pupils' book to help you complete this worksheet by filling in the spaces.

The Council

The four permanent members _____ ,
_____ , _____ ,
_____ could veto
decisions. There were also non-permanent
members. Votes had to be _____
_____ .

The Assembly

All members had _____ vote.
It recommended action to the Council. Votes
had to be _____ .

The Secretariat

This was a kind of _____
_____
_____ .

Permanent Court of International Justice

Based at The _____ .

Both countries had to request a decision from
the court.

Commissions and Agencies

I _____
L _____
O _____
Aim: to improve
_____
_____
_____
_____

Mandates Commission

Aim: to oversee
_____
_____
_____
_____
_____

Minorities Commission

Aim: to protect
_____
_____
_____
_____
_____

Other Agencies

Examples:
_____
_____
_____
_____
_____

Complete the following sentences:

1 The idea of Collective Security was _____

2 The Covenant of the League was _____

3 The right of veto was held by _____

4 Mandates were _____

5 The headquarters of the League were in _____

Explain how one of the weaknesses shown on page 50 could weaken the League.

_____

_____

_____

Which of the members might consider the weaknesses to be strengths and why?

_____

_____

_____

 **The League of Nations – Powers, weaknesses and strengths**

What were the League's strengths and weaknesses?

Use pages 48–51 of the pupils' book to fill in the spaces.

Aim: _____

Weaknesses

The League was seen as a

_____

_____

The League was tied in with the Peace Treaties which were hated by some countries, e.g.

_____

_____

There were weaknesses in the League's organisation, e.g. (see Worksheet 18)

_____

_____

Some powerful countries only belonged for short periods, e.g.

_____

_____

The most powerful country, the

_____,

never joined.

Powers of the League

— 1st
Moral
condemnation

— 2nd
Economic
sanctions

— 3rd
Military force
(but not its own)

Strengths

44 nations joined.

But the USA did not join.

The horrors of the war meant most people supported the League.

But these memories were to fade.

The powers of the League were strong if used well.

But they were not well used in the 1930s.

It was much less dangerous than the old way of keeping peace – the Alliance System.

1 Do you think the League will stand or fall?

2 What do you think is the key weakness?

3 What do you think is the key strength?

20 *The League of Nations in the 1920s*

How successful was the League in the 1920s?

Use pages 52–55 of the pupils' book to complete this chart on the disputes and problems tackled by the League.

Dispute/ problem	Dispute between	What was the problem?	Success/ Failure
1919 Vilna			
Aaland Islands 1920			
Upper Silesia 1920			
Russia 1920–22			
Yugoslavia and Albania 1921			
The economies of Austria and Hungary 1922–23			
Disarmament			

1 Use page 54 to explain how the disputes between Greece and Bulgaria, and Greece and Italy were in one way similar but in another way different.

2 Explain in approximately 100 words how successful the League was in dealing with problems in the 1920s.

21 *The League of Nations and Abyssinia*

How did the League tackle the Abyssinian crisis?

Use pages 66–68 of the pupils' book to help you complete this worksheet.

In 1935 the Italian dictator, _____ ,
ordered his troops to invade Abyssinia. He wanted to extend Italy's Empire
and wanted revenge for an Italian defeat at the battle of _____
in 1896. Abyssinia was ruled by _____ _____
and was a member of the _____ _____ _____ .
Abyssinia was surrounded by the colonies of European powers. The Italian
colonies of _____ and _____ _____
bordered Abyssinia.

   This invasion posed a serious problem for the League of Nations as it
would show if the idea of _____ security was going
to work. It also threatened to break up the '_____ Front' of
Britain, France and _____ , formed to stand against the growing
power of Germany. If Britain and France, the leading members of the
League, opposed the invasion then Italy could leave the '_____
Front' and ally with Germany.

   The League did oppose the invasion and applied weak
_____ sanctions against Italy. But these did not
include vital items such as steel, _____ or _____ .
In December 1935 there was a secret attempt by Britain and France to
make a deal with Italy by allowing them to keep part of Abyssinia. This was
called the _____ _____ Plan. When the public
found out about the plan it was so unpopular it had to be dropped.

   Italy won the war and the League had failed.

The consequences for the League were serious:

1 As a peacekeeping organisation it had _____ .

2 Mussolini was encouraged to become involved in the Spanish _____ _____ .

3 Italy left the League and allied with _____ in the Rome-Berlin Axis, and
then joined the _____ Pact.

22 Steps to war 1933–39 (1)

How should other leaders react to Hitler?

This chart is to help you keep a record of your decisions in this section of the pupils' book (pages 72–86). Remember your aims are to stop Hitler if you think he is wrong and to avoid war.

	Your advice	**Was your advice the same as the action taken by Britain and France? Yes/No/Partly**	**Were Hitler's demands reasonable? Why?**
Decision 1 Rearmament 1933			
Decision 2 The Rhineland 1936 Advice to Britain			
Advice to France			
Decision 3 Austria			
Decision 4 Czechoslovakia			
Decision 5 Poland			
Decision 6 Hitler's offer or war?			

1 If you think that most of Hitler's demands were reasonable, do you think the Treaty of Versailles was unfair?

2 Do you think you made a wrong decision at any point?

3 Do you think Britain and France made a wrong decision at any point?

4 Was it possible to avoid war?

5 In approximately 100 words write your own account of the steps to war.

Key History for GCSE: International Relations 1919–39 – Teacher's Guide © Stanley Thornes (Publishers) Ltd. 1998

How did the war in Europe come about?

Complete this worksheet using pages 72–87 to help you.

When Hitler became leader of _____ his aim was to reverse the Treaty of

_____ . He also wanted to unite all Germans in a single

_____ and win _____ by invading Russia and

_____ . He began by rearming Germany.

In 1934 he wanted to reunite Germany and Austria but the opposition of

_____ stopped this. In 1935 the _____ area voted

to return to German control. The leaders of Italy, France and _____ were worried

by the growing strength of Germany and so formed the _____ Front to stand together

against Germany. But this was soon in trouble. First Britain upset France by signing the

_____ _____ _____ Treaty. Then in 1936 Italy fell out with Britain and

France because they opposed Italy's invasion of _____ .

Hitler's next success was in 1936 when his troops reoccupied the _____ area of

Germany which had been demilitarised at Versailles. This made it much more difficult to enforce the

Versailles Treaty on Germany. Hitler had also broken promises Germany had made in the

_____ Pact signed in 1925.

In 1936 Hitler tested German troops and weapons when he sent help to General Franco in the

_____ Civil War. Germany also signed the Anti-Comintern Pact with Japan and

_____ .

In 1938 Hitler bullied the Austrian leader, _____ , into agreeing to the

_____ , (the union of Germany and Austria).

Hitler was now well placed to achieve his next aim and destroy Czechoslovakia. Three million

_____ Germans lived in Czechoslovakia near the German border. Hitler

demanded the Sudetenland become part of Germany. But Czechoslovakia had a modern army and was

protected by fortifications. Also _____ had promised military help if Germany

attacked Czechoslovakia.

Hitler used the Sudeten Nazis to stir up trouble and war seemed likely. Britain and France wanted to

avoid war and followed a policy of _____ . In September 1938 three meetings took

place between Hitler and the British Prime Minister _____

_____ . The final meeting was held at _____ and it was

agreed by Germany, Britain, _____ and _____ that

Germany could take the Sudetenland.

Hitler's next target was _____ . Chamberlain now decided Germany must be

stopped and gave a guarantee to stand by _____ . But Hitler signed the

_____ _____ Pact with _____ in

which he agreed to divide Poland with Soviet Russia. On _____ Germany invaded

Poland and _____ days later Britain and _____ declared war on

Germany.

24 The fall of Czechoslovakia

Why was the Munich Agreement fatal for Czechoslovakia?

The Czechs were deserted at Munich and had no choice but to accept Hitler's terms. The Munich Agreement greatly weakened Czechoslovakia.

Source **A** on page 78 of the pupils' book shows the territory Czechoslovakia lost to her neighbours. The map below shows what resources and defences were lost because of the Munich Agreement. Study both maps carefully and answer the questions below.

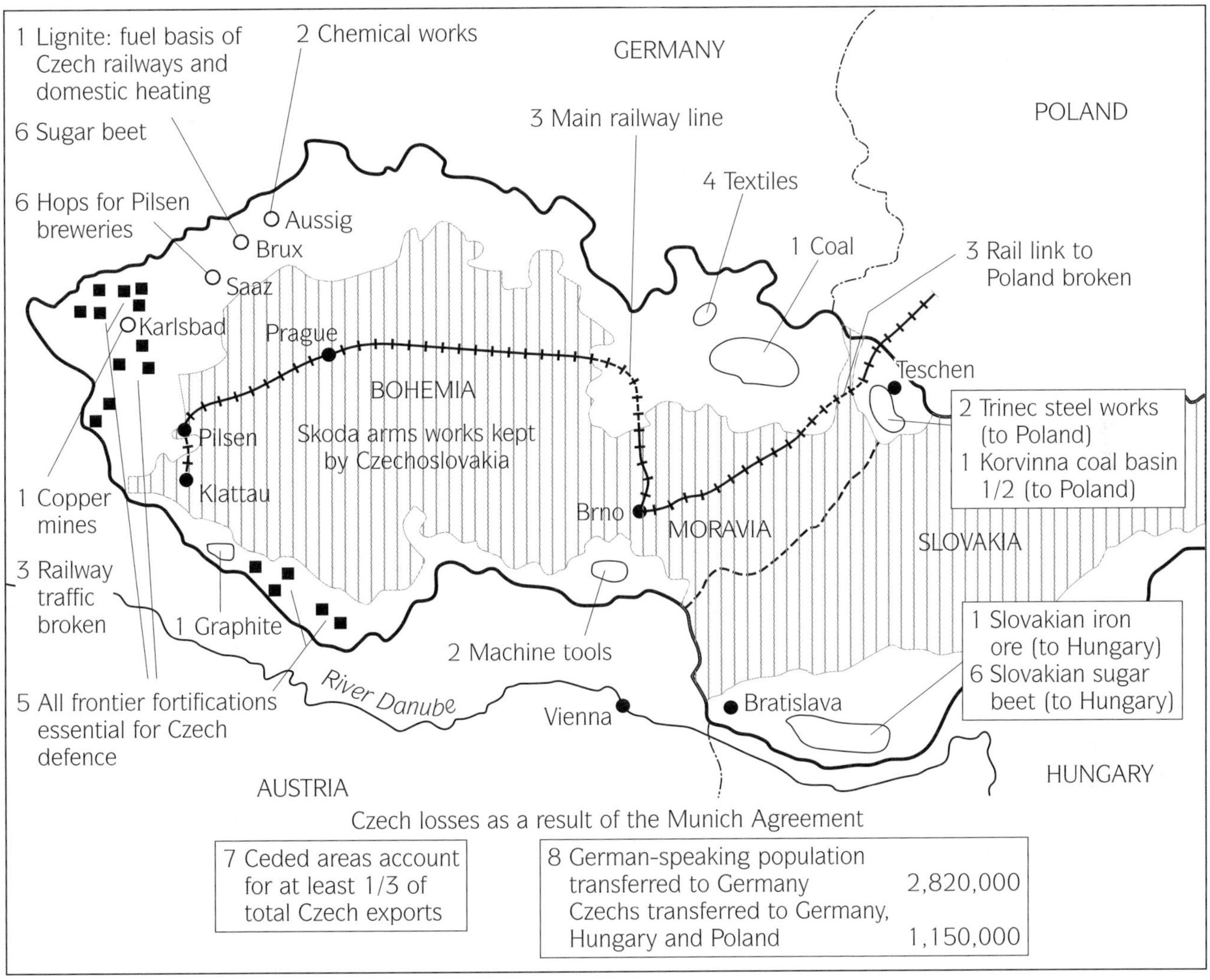

1 Lignite: fuel basis of Czech railways and domestic heating

2 Chemical works

GERMANY

6 Sugar beet

3 Main railway line

POLAND

6 Hops for Pilsen breweries

4 Textiles

Aussig
Brux
Saaz

1 Coal

3 Rail link to Poland broken

Karlsbad
Prague

BOHEMIA

Teschen

2 Trinec steel works (to Poland)
1 Korvinna coal basin 1/2 (to Poland)

Pilsen
Klattau

Skoda arms works kept by Czechoslovakia

Brno
MORAVIA

SLOVAKIA

1 Copper mines

3 Railway traffic broken

1 Graphite

2 Machine tools

1 Slovakian iron ore (to Hungary)
6 Slovakian sugar beet (to Hungary)

5 All frontier fortifications essential for Czech defence

River Danube

Vienna

Bratislava

HUNGARY

AUSTRIA

Czech losses as a result of the Munich Agreement

7 Ceded areas account for at least 1/3 of total Czech exports	8 German-speaking population transferred to Germany	2,820,000
	Czechs transferred to Germany, Hungary and Poland	1,150,000

Key

1–8 are different types of resources lost by Czechoslovakia:
1 = minerals
2 = industrial plants
3 = railways
4 = textiles
5 = defences
6 = agricultural crops
7 = exports
8 = population

1 For each resource, 1–8, explain how its loss weakened Czechoslovakia.

2 Decide which of the resources, 1–8, is the most serious loss.

3 Name three ways in which it was now more difficult for Czechoslovakia to defend herself.

4 What other information do you need about Czechoslovakia to decide if she is still a viable country?

25 Appeasement

Was appeasement wrong or was it a sensible policy?

This worksheet provides a framework to help you compare the two sets of arguments on page 82 of the pupils' book. First compare arguments 1–6 and tick the column you most agree with. Then look at arguments 7–11, if you accept the argument and think it is an important point then tick the correct column.

The Arguments

	✓	Appeasement was wrong	OR	Appeasement was sensible	✓
1		Hitler's aims were clear and Chamberlain was fooled.		Germany's early demands were reasonable and if accepted then Germany might have been satisfied.	
2		German armed forces were not as strong as Britain thought. Appeasement gave Hitler time to strengthen his forces.		The German army and airforce were superior to Britain's, time was needed to rearm.	
3		The French army was the strongest in Europe.		The French army was organised only to defend France.	
4		The Czech army was modern.		The Czech army was divided.	
5		The German airforce could not launch a serious attack on Britain.		Britain had no real air defence.	
6		Russia appeared ready to help Czechoslovakia.		Russia was communist and could not be relied on.	
7		Appeasement made France's allies – Yugoslavia and Romania – lose confidence.			
8		It was dishonourable to desert Czechoslovakia.			
9				Most of the British Empire were not prepared to fight for Czechoslovakia.	
10				War in Europe would mean Japan could threaten Britain's Empire in the Far East.	
11				The British public did not want to go to war over Czechoslovakia.	

1 Do you think appeasement was wrong or sensible?

2 Which of the following statements do you accept?

  a) The column with the most ticks represents my view of appeasement.

  b) Some of the arguments are more important than others, it is not simply the number of ticks which is important.

3 Which arguments do you think are the most important?

Key History for GCSE: International Relations 1919–39 – Teacher's Guide © Stanley Thornes (Publishers) Ltd. 1998

26 The Nazi-Soviet Pact

Why did Hitler and Stalin sign the Pact?

Complete this worksheet by filling in the spaces and completing the sentences. Use pages 84–86 of the pupils' book to help you.

On 23 August Germany and Soviet Russia signed a non-aggression pact.

Hitler and Stalin agreed to _____

_____

_____

_____

Hitler signed the Pact because _____

_____

_____

The reasons why Stalin signed the Pact include:

1 When Stalin suggested a treaty with Britain and France it was six weeks

  before _____

  _____

2 Stalin feared _____

  _____

3 Stalin thought Britain and France were not serious about a treaty because

  _____

4 The Battle of _____

5 Poland refused _____

  _____

6 On 23 August Ribbentrop, the German foreign minister,

  _____

7 The Pact with Germany offered _____

  _____

  _____

8 An alliance with Britain and France would probably mean _____

  Also the British army _____

  The French army _____

  The Nazi-Soviet Pact made it possible for Hitler to invade

  _____ and avoid a war on two _____ as

  Russia would remain neutral. Hitler did not expect Britain and

  _____ to stand by their guarantee to help Poland if

she was invaded.

27 The causes of war – Interpretations

Why did war break out in Europe? Do historians agree?

This is a copy of Source **A** on page 88 of the pupils' book to help you complete the task at the top of page 89.

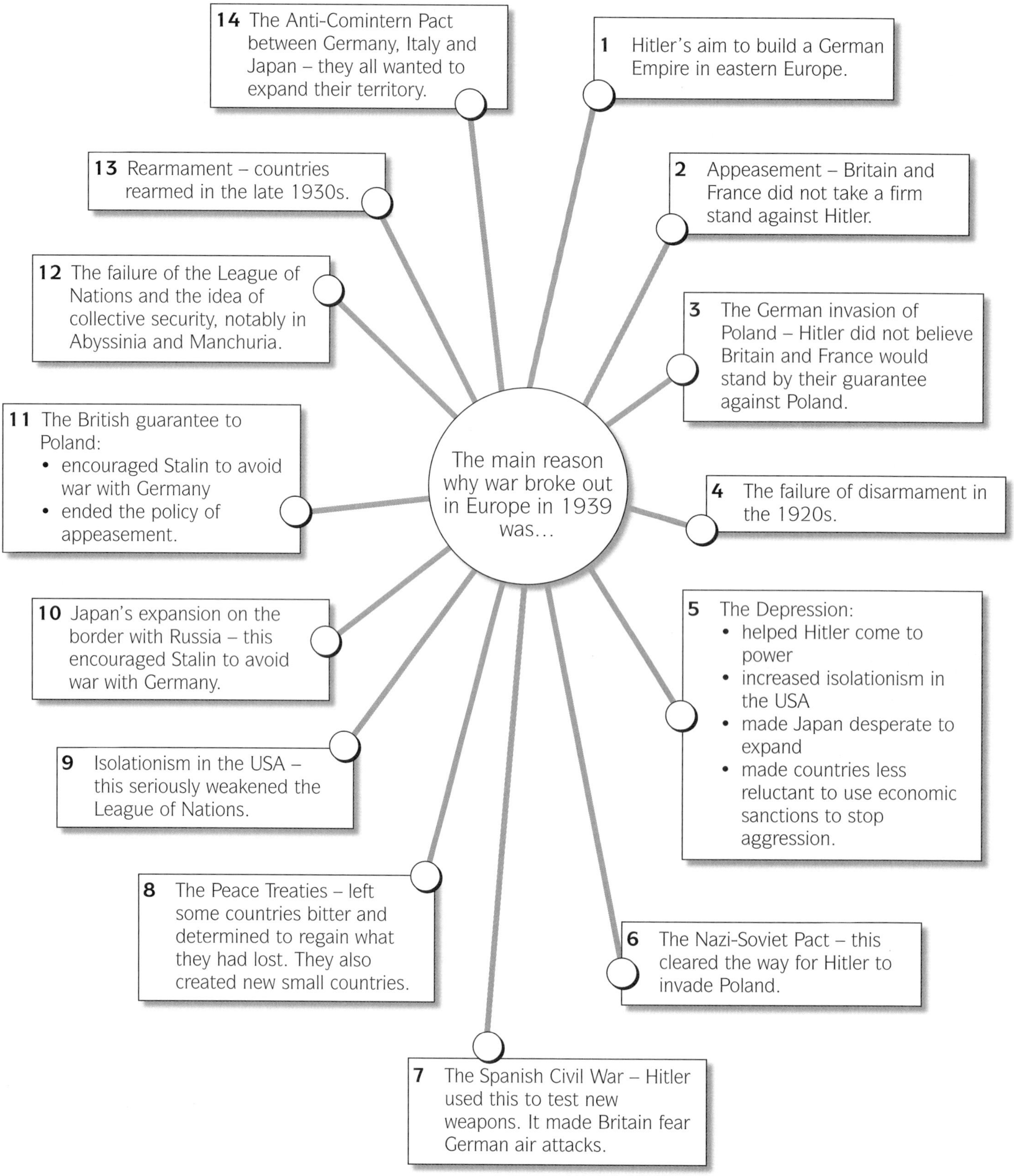

14 The Anti-Comintern Pact between Germany, Italy and Japan – they all wanted to expand their territory.

1 Hitler's aim to build a German Empire in eastern Europe.

13 Rearmament – countries rearmed in the late 1930s.

2 Appeasement – Britain and France did not take a firm stand against Hitler.

12 The failure of the League of Nations and the idea of collective security, notably in Abyssinia and Manchuria.

3 The German invasion of Poland – Hitler did not believe Britain and France would stand by their guarantee against Poland.

11 The British guarantee to Poland:
• encouraged Stalin to avoid war with Germany
• ended the policy of appeasement.

The main reason why war broke out in Europe in 1939 was…

4 The failure of disarmament in the 1920s.

5 The Depression:
• helped Hitler come to power
• increased isolationism in the USA
• made Japan desperate to expand
• made countries less reluctant to use economic sanctions to stop aggression.

10 Japan's expansion on the border with Russia – this encouraged Stalin to avoid war with Germany.

9 Isolationism in the USA – this seriously weakened the League of Nations.

8 The Peace Treaties – left some countries bitter and determined to regain what they had lost. They also created new small countries.

6 The Nazi-Soviet Pact – this cleared the way for Hitler to invade Poland.

7 The Spanish Civil War – Hitler used this to test new weapons. It made Britain fear German air attacks.

28 ◢ The causes of war

Did the two World Wars have similar causes?

This worksheet is to help with the difficult task of comparing the causes of war in 1939 with the causes of war in 1914. The causes of war in 1914 are outlined on pages 10–11 of your pupils' book and are shown below on the left. In the column on the right enter what you believe are the main causes of war in 1939 – use pages 88–89 of the pupils' book to help you.

Causes of war in 1914	Causes of war in 1939
The rise of Germany When Germany was united in 1870–71 she quickly became the most powerful state on the continent. The Kaiser wanted Germany to build an empire and so built up his navy and army.	
The Arms Race Other powers tried to match the growing power of Germany's army and navy. Britain expanded her navy and France and Russia increased their armies.	
Problems in the Austro-Hungarian Empire This was struggling to control the different national groups it contained. It wanted to defeat Serbia to contain this problem.	
The problem of Empire Germany wanted an empire like the other great European powers, this caused tension with Britain and France.	
The Alliance System Europe was divided into two alliance systems, so when conflict began between two members of different alliances the other countries quickly became involved.	

Now complete the following sentences:

The causes of war in 1914 and 1939 had similarities and differences. The similarities were _____

_____

_____

_____

The differences were _____

_____

_____

_____

29A *World peace 1919–39*

When did the threat to peace become serious?

When did war become likely?

Changes in the eight factors listed on the following two pages indicate whether world peace was stronger or under threat. Complete the chart by showing changes in the years 1920–29, 1930–38, and 1939.

Complete each sentence to summarise the change. Then extend the arrow to the date you think the statement still applies. The first factor is partly completed.

Factor	1920–29	1930–38	1939
League of Nations – success or failure?	Several key successes, e.g. the Aaland Islands	Crucial failures, e.g. Abyssinia	Irrelevant to world peace

This shows the League had successes in the 1920s but failed to settle international disputes in the 1930s.

The League was more a success than a failure

——————————————————➤

Factor	1920–29	1930–38	1939
Disarmament – progress towards.	Germany was disarmed but…	?	?

This shows

Disarmament was being achieved.

– – – ➤

Factor	1920–29	1930–38	1939
Rise of Fascism	The first Fascist country was …	Both Italy and…	?

This shows

Fascist countries were not a threat.

– – – ➤

Factor	1920–29	1930–38	1939
Wars	Poland and Russia…	In 1936 Spain…	?

This shows

Wars did not threaten world peace.

– – – ➤

Factor	1920–29	1930–38	1939
The policy of the USA	The USA decided on a policy of...	?	?

This shows

The USA took no part in helping to keep world peace.

━ ━ ━ ➤

Factor	1920–29	1930–38	1939
Japan's relations with her neighbours.	?	At war with...	?

This shows

Japan was at peace with her neighbours.

━ ━ ━ ➤

Factor	1920–29	1930–38	1939
British foreign policy	At the League she supported...	Increasingly she adopted a policy of...	?

This shows

Britain's support of the League helped keep peace.

━ ━ ━ ➤

Factor	1920–29	1930–38	1939
Economic problems threatened peace	War debts and reparations...	The Depression...	?

This shows

Economic problems did *not* damage relations between countries.

━ ━ ━ ➤

1 When was the turning point during the inter-war years when the threat to peace became serious? Can you pin it down to one year?

2 How many years later did war become likely?

3 Which of the eight factors do you think was the most important?

30 *Russia and international relations 1919–41*

How did Soviet Russia's policy change?

Complete the following sentences about Russia's relations with the world choosing the correct words from the brackets. Some page numbers are given to help you.

1917–19 The new state of Communist Russia led by Lenin fought a civil war in which the anti-Communists in Russia were helped by troops from _____ [Britain, France, USA, Japan, Germany, Poland].

1917 Relations with capitalist countries _____ [were/were not] helped when Lenin set up the Comintern to help _____ [defeat/spread] Communist ideas.

1920–23 Poland and Russia fought a war which Russia _____ [won/lost].

1922 The Treaty of Rapallo meant relations with _____ [Germany/Britain] improved. (Page 32.)

1929–34 Russia _____ [was/was not] a member of the League of Nations.

1920s Russia _____ [did/did not] trust capitalism.

1928 The new Soviet leader Stalin believed Russia _____ [should/should not] improve relations with other countries and _____ [signed/did not sign] the Kellogg-Briand Pact.

1929–30 Because Russia was a communist country the effect of the Depression on the Russian economy was _____ [more severe/less severe] than on most countries. (Page 58.)

1930s Stalin used the Comintern for _____ [stirring up world revolution/spying and spreading propaganda]. (Page 43.)

1930s Increasingly Japan was a new _____ [friend/threat] to Russia.

1934 Russia joined the League of Nations because Stalin saw the rise of Fascism as a _____ [threat/friend] to Communism. Fascism and Communism had _____ [similar/different] aims and _____ [similar/different] methods. (Pages 8–9.)

1936 Russia was _____ [concerned/reassured] when Germany and Japan signed the Anti-Comintern Pact.

1938 Russia was _____ [angry/happy] when Britain, France, Germany and Italy signed the Munich Agreement. It seemed a good reason to _____ [trust/distrust] these countries.

1939 Stalin signed the Nazi-Soviet Pact with Germany because he feared a war on two fronts against _____ [China/Japan] in the East, and against _____ [Germany/Britain] in the West. Also Stalin did not trust Chamberlain who he believed was trying to push _____ [Germany/Poland] to attack Russia. (Page 85.)

1941 June 'Operation Barbarossa' meant Germany and Russia were _____ [at war/allies] and relations between Russia and Britain, France and the USA _____ [improved/deteriorated].

31 *The USA and international relations 1919–41*

How did American policy change?

Complete the following sentences about America's relations with the world, choosing the correct words from the brackets. Some page numbers are given to help you.

1914   The USA _____ [was/was not] allied to a European power and entered the war in 1917.

1915   The American President, Woodrow Wilson, believed the war had been fought _____ [for/against] democracy. He _____ [wanted/did not want] to humiliate Germany and so wanted the peace to be based on his Fourteen Points.

1919   The USA had loaned huge sums of money to the victorious allies and _____ [did/did not] want these repaid.

1920   The American Senate _____ [agreed/refused] to ratify the Treaty of Versailles. Many Americans thought the Treaty too _____ [harsh/lenient] on Germany. The USA also _____ [agreed/refused] to join the League of Nations. (Pages 38–39.)

1920   The Presidential election was won by _____ [Wilson/Harding] so there _____ [was/was not] a chance the USA might change its mind. America now followed a policy of _____ [isolationism/involvement].

1921–22   The USA signed the Washington Naval Treaties which agreed to _____ [limit/increase] the size of the navies of the great powers. The American navy was to be the _____ [largest/equal largest]. (Page 32.)

1924   American banks _____ [did/did not] lend money to European countries under the Dawes Plan. America was _____ [keen/unwilling] to import European goods so Europe's recovery from the war was _____ [slow/quick]. (Page 32.)

1928   The USA signed the Kellogg-Briand Pact which _____ [renounced/supported] the use of war to settle international disputes.

1929   The American stock market on Wall Street _____ [crashed/boomed] and a world depression began. This pushed America further _____ [into/out of] isolation.

1931   America _____ [was/was not] a member of the League of Nations and this made it _____ [easier/more difficult] for the League to deal with Japan's invasion of Manchuria.

1935 & 1937   America passed neutrality laws which _____ [prevented/allowed] America to trade with countries involved in a war.

1939   When war broke out in Europe opinion in America began to change. The American President, Roosevelt, warned that _____ [democracy/fascism] was threatened by Germany and Italy. The law was changed so that America _____ [could/could not] sell arms to Britain and France.

1941   The Lend-lease Plan was passed to allow America to 'lend' war supplies to _____ [Britain/Germany].

1941   America was increasingly worried by _____ [Japanese/Chinese] aggression in the Far East and stopped exports of _____ [oil/rice] to Japan. Then on 7 December Japan attacked the American naval base at Pearl Harbor and the two countries were at war. (Pages 92–94.)

32 *Japan and international relations 1919–41*

How did Japanese policy change?

Complete the following sentences about Japan's relations with the world, choosing the correct words from the brackets. Some page numbers are given to help you.

1919 Japan had been on the _____ [winning/losing] side in the First World War. She gained _____ [Germany's/France's] colonies in the Far East but was dissatisfied with this.

1920s Japan was the most powerful country in the Far East and she wanted to build an empire. She _____ [disliked/liked] the power of the Western Powers in the area and wanted to change this.

1921–22 Japan agreed to the Washington Naval Treaties in which she agreed to limit the size of her _____ [navy/army] and not to invade _____ [China/Russia]. (Page 32.)

1929 The World Depression hit Japan hard. The value of her main export _____ [silk/rice] fell sharply. She needed more raw materials for her industries and food for her population but she could not afford to import these. She believed she would find these by invading _____ [Korea/Manchuria]. (Pages 46–47.)

1931 Manchuria was part of China but the South Manchurian Railway was owned by _____ [Britain/Japan]. They said it was under attack and used this as an excuse to invade Manchuria. China appealed to the League of Nations. The League's response was _____ [weak/strong] and Japan _____ [left/joined] the League. (Pages 64–65.)

1936 Japan signed the Anti-Comintern Pact with _____ [Russia/Germany]. This was an alliance against _____ [Communism/Fascism].

1930s In Japan the _____ [army/peasants] had great power and wanted to invade more of China.

1937 Japan invaded most of north-east China. It was a very brutal invasion. China appealed to the League of Nations which _____ [condemned/approved] the invasion. The League was _____ [powerful/powerless]. The only country with the power to stop Japan was _____ [Britain/the USA] but she did not want to endanger her trade with Japan.

1938 Japan announced a 'New Order in East Asia', this was to lead to the removal of _____ [Western/Russian] influence, instead Japan would be in control of the area.

1941 Germany was Japan's ally, when Germany attacked Russia Japan _____ [refused/agreed] to join the attack. Instead she wanted to expand _____ [southwards/northwards], but this would bring her into conflict with the USA and Britain.

The USA was worried by the growing power of Japan and demanded Japan withdraw from _____ [China/Russia]. The USA, Britain and the Netherlands were already refusing to sell oil to Japan.

1941 The Japanese Prime Minister, General Tojo, believed Japan had to fight to survive. In an attempt to knockout the _____ [American/British] fleet, Japan attacked the naval base at Pearl Harbor without warning. The USA declared war on Japan. The world was now at war.

33 Timeline between the wars

What were the links between the two World Wars?

Britain, France and the USA signed the Treaty of Versailles with Germany in June 1919. On 3 September 1939 Britain and France declared war on Germany. The boxes on this worksheet show key events between these two World Wars.

1 Cut out the events and use the index in the pupils' book to find out the date of each event. Then arrange them in the correct sequence to make your own timeline.

2 Most of the events can be linked to the First World War and to the Second World War. Divide a sheet of paper into three columns. Head the first column 'First World War', the second column 'Timeline 1917–1939', and the third column 'Second World War'. Copy out your timeline in the middle column. Then discuss with your neighbour how each of the events can be linked to the two World Wars and write your links in the correct column alongside each event.

Treaty of Versailles	Japan attacks Pearl Harbor	Hitler comes to power in Germany
Communist revolution in Russia	Germany invades Poland	Locarno Treaties
Germany invades the Sudetenland	The League of Nations formed	Japan invades Manchuria
Wall Street crashes and the Depression begins	Munich Conference	Nazi-Soviet Non-Aggression Pact
Japan invades north-east China	Italy invades Abyssinia	Germany achieves the Anschluss (union with Austria)
Germany reoccupies the Rhineland		

Key History for GCSE: International Relations 1919–39 – Teacher's Guide © Stanley Thornes (Publishers) Ltd. 1998

34 *Hitler's responsibility*

How far was Hitler to blame for the war?

Historians disagree on how far Hitler was responsible for causing the Second World War.

View one

Historians such as Winston Churchill and E H Carr believe that Hitler had a long term plan to bring about German domination of Europe. This was set out in Hitler's autobiography *Mein Kampf* which made it clear Hitler wanted to gather all the scattered pockets of Germans in Europe into a great German Empire. Also Germany needed more land in Eastern Europe. If necessary Hitler would use force to achieve these aims.

The steps in this policy were clear: rearmament, re-militarisation of the Rhineland, the take-over of Austria, the invasion of Czechoslovakia, the invasion of Poland.

View two

The historian A J P Taylor argues that Hitler had no plan but simply made the best of opportunities presented by the other powers to reunite Germans and tear up the Treaty of Versailles? When war came it was because Hitler miscalculated the reactions of Britain and France to the crisis he had deliberately created over Poland. *Mein Kampf* was merely the dreams of a failed revolutionary.

Some recent historians have argued a middle course between these two views.

If Hitler had a master plan and was preparing for war, then he must take most or all of the blame for causing the war. But if war was caused by a miscalculation by Hitler, partly due to the behaviour of Britain and France, then maybe less blame should be put on Hitler.

Consider the following statements and decide if they support either of the two views:

1 Hitler adopted an aggressive style in his conduct of foreign policy.
2 Hitler stressed the need for Lebensraum, living space, in Eastern Europe.
3 The German demands for access across the Polish Corridor were reasonable, but Poland refused to consider them. The British guarantee to Poland encouraged Poland not to negotiate.
4 The Nazi-Soviet Pact contained secret clauses to divide Poland between Germany and Russia.
5 Hitler failed to understand how his breaking of the Munich Agreement by invading the rest of Czechoslovakia changed opinion in Britain and ended the policy of appeasement.
6 Britain could not enforce the guarantee given to Poland.

The final two statements concern a vital piece of evidence – the Hossbach Memorandum.
In November 1937 Colonel Hossbach wrote notes of a meeting he attended between Hitler and his top officials and generals. Hossbach wrote that Hitler said his aim was to win living space and he would need to use force to do this. Is this evidence of a master plan?

7 Hossbach wrote his account from memory five days later, the only surviving version is a copy of a copy of the original.
8 There is no serious reason to doubt the accuracy of the Memorandum. It says that Hitler warned that Germany would not be fully prepared for war until the mid 1940s but she could not wait that long and must take advantage of any opportunity before that date. This is almost exactly what happened.

How far do you think Hitler was to blame for the war?